RIVER OF TRAPS

University of New Mexico Press

in association with
the Center for Documentary Studies
at Duke University

William deBuys
and Alex Harris

RIVER OF TRAPS

A Village Life

With the exception of Jacobo Romero and his family, Tomás Montoya, public figures, and the authors and their families, the names of many characters and certain details have been altered to protect the privacy of individuals. Additionally, some of the characters and events described in Chapter 8 are drawn from outside the village of El Valle.

Chapters 1 and 2 of *River of Traps* originally appeared in the *Southwest Review*.

Text copyright © 1990 by William deBuys. All rights reserved.
Photographs copyright © 1990 by Alex Harris. All rights reserved.
Second printing, 1990
Library of Congress Cataloging-in-Publication Data

DeBuys, William Eno.
    River of traps: a village life / William DeBuys and Alex Harris.
        p.   cm.
    Includes bibliographical references.
    ISBN 0-8263-1182-2
    1. Sangre de Cristo Mountains (Colo. and N.M.)—Social life and customs.
    2. Sangre de Cristo Mountains (Colo. and N.M.)—Biography.
    3. Romero, Jacobo.
    4. DeBuys, William Eno.
    5. Harris, Alex, 1949–   .
    I. Harris, Alex, 1949–   .
    II. Title.
F802.S35D44   1990
978.9'5—dc20   89-25085

Contents

Greeting Canto   8

1. The Shovel Is A Tool of Art   11

2. Water Will Show   27

Sunset Canto   40

3. The Right Place   43

4. Diamante   51

5. Travels Without Maps   69

Walking Canto   86

6. Intactness   89

Field Canto   106

7. The Society Is Losing Our Mind   109

8. The Body Politic   119

9. Red Horse   131

10. Gringismo   145

Woodpile Canto   164

11. Retratos   167

12. River of Traps   185

13. The Bird of the Bleeding Throat   201

Fence Canto   216

14. Preparation   219

Feeding Canto   232

Acknowledgements   237

for Robert Coles

Greeting Canto

. . . summer afternoon, dust boils behind the big RV. The campground isn't far.

Here at last are the green mountains, the cool river, the rustic homes beside the fields, and the forest beyond.

An old mexicano *shoes a gaunt red horse beside the road. He files a hoof and puts it down and stands to stretch his back. The horse drowses, as still as death.*

The old man smiles at the passers-by and tips his hat. From the air-conditioned cab they see his lips move in greeting.

They wave and return the welcoming smile. Such a kind old man, white-haired and strong-featured, shoeing his horse by an adobe house at the end of a long and crooked journey.

Here is the tan of the road, the red of the horse, the gray of the peaks in the distance. Here, surrounded by forest, lies the ancient village. The tableau is complete.

The old man waves and again his lips move. The tourists rumble past, dust billowing. They do not hear what he says. They do not hear the wry, self-mocking irony.

The old man grins and waves and calls his invitation: "¡Come mierda!"

He waves again: "¡Come chite!"

His smile is all innocence, as broad as kindness. And the tourists smile back, waving through the glass.

Welcome! Though appearances deceive.

Welcome! To you who are part of what you see.

The RV growls into the distance, dust settles, and the old man turns to the horse, savoring his deception. He mutters, grinning to no one, "Come mierda, come chite," *and the file rasps against the hoof.*

1

The Shovel Is a Tool of Art

We lived at the bottom of the village where the river squeezed between two hills and vanished in a canyon. The river was a small one, too small to be called a river in most parts of the world, but clear and cold, and we soon learned not to take its size as the measure of its power. In summer the cottonwoods that grew along its banks rang with the chatter of small birds, and up the slope, inside a wire fence that sagged from the straining of hungry cattle, ravens and magpies came every day to strut through the wet places of our hayfield. We had those wet places because we were lowest on the irrigation ditch, and it was our practice to leave our water gates open, even when it was not our turn to irrigate, in order to capture what leaked down to us from neighbors upstream.

The ditch ran for over a mile through the village, and like other ditches farther up the valley, it carried the lifeblood of the village in fair weather and its leftovers and lost things in foul. According to ancient custom, everyone who irrigated was obliged, no matter how thirsty his fields, to leave a small amount of water in the ditch for the household needs and livestock of people farther down, but since no one lived below us, we were free to use this small amount of water as we wished. We made the trickle run into the field not so much to coax an extra half-bale from the timothy as to keep the regard of the old man who was our closest neighbor and who taught us what we knew of irrigation. He chided us relentlessly never to "give holiday to the water" but to put every drop to work. Obediently, we kept our gates open to the field, and there were times following wild thunderstorms when we went out into the bending hay to find live trout, whole beers, or forgotten laundry washed down to us by the ditch. More than once we found faded plastic flowers from the graveyard.

The *camposanto* and our land lay on opposite sides of the same scrubby hill. Coming into the village from the paved highway, you drove two miles on dirt through dust-clad pines and juniper. The graveyard was the first sign of the village you saw. Protected by a pigwire fence on stout cedar posts, the three or four dozen graves lay in even ranks, feet to the road. Some were boxed by small picket fences; most had plastic flowers.

Except when sunflowers sprout from July rains, the graveyard grows no real flowers. It grows white wooden crosses, granite headstones, and plastic bouquets, but nothing that blooms. Its fine-grained clay, pale as tender skin, turns greasy in the rain and dries brittle. And clay is all there is. There is no duff, no humus to nourish a seed or deny moisture to the air. The only dressing on the soil is a thin pavement of pebbles, which erosion has left behind. We used to joke when we dug a grave that in our *camposanto* the usual layering of soils was upside down. All the organic matter lay six feet under.

On anniversaries of birth and death, Memorial Days, and the like, the people of the village decorate the graves of their loved ones with plastic flowers as brilliantly colored as new cars. Blue roses, orange chrysanthemums, wine-red zinnias. When last year's flowers have faded in the sun, new ones appear on the tidy graves, and the old are cast beyond the pigwire to lie for months, or years, in the shadow of low trees, where ants and horned toads roam over them. With time, the sun bleaches them to a milky opacity, and the rain and wind thinly bury their everlasting leaves.

Inevitably, there comes a storm that so drenches the hillside that the surface of the ground itself begins to flow, and the flowers wash away. The water peels them from the hillside in a paste of soil. They roll into the ditch that runs beside the road; they sluice down the ditch and into an arroyo, swirling around old bed springs and over an ancient stove; they sweep past a tangle of roots and into the roiling chocolate water of the irrigation ditch, finally to flush into our field.

We collected those flowers and twined them in the branches of the junipers that lined the ditch. One particular white rose hung in the big juniper by the first water gate for at least ten years. I remember putting it there, soon after we bought the land, on a cold spring morning when the old man undertook to teach us the art of irrigation.

The knowledge we needed was basic to tending our land, and it was simple compared to irrigating plowed land. We had only to spread our water over a tight sod of pasture grasses and to manage its descent down the slope of the field. The object was to give all the land a good drink while permitting none of it to erode.

But the slope was considerable, and at the fence the land broke still more steeply toward the river. There were gullies where the slope changed, not large ones, but raw as wounds. When we imagined ourselves setting loose the water to run through the field for a night, we saw those gullies grow to chasms, gouging scars in our new land.

Our fear was the worse because we recognized we were disadvantaged as irrigators. We lacked experience in handling water, and worse, our backs and arms had little education. In our hands a shovel was a clumsy tool, to say nothing of an axe or an iron digging bar.

We were three: Alex, Anne, and me. We had come to the village several years before, by various routes and for various reasons. Alex's were mainly artistic, though he didn't much talk about them. He was a photographer, just starting out, and quiet by nature. Once he mentioned that the mountains kept a person far enough away from critics and curators that he didn't have to struggle not to hear them. It was easy to see how Alex was drawn to the mountain people and to the landscape. The way they fit together made him feel both comfortable and charged up. I thought of him in those days as being almost an innocent. Anywhere but in the mountains, I wondered if he'd be all right.

Anne and I also had artistic aspirations. She painted landscapes and still lifes that were meticulous and deeply felt. Her colors were as clean as the land and possessed a clarity that grew stronger the longer we lived there. I, meanwhile, was writing a book, though for a long time I wasn't sure about what, except that the mountains had to figure in it. The high country was my anchor, solid and constant. I wrote in my journal that the years of Nixon and Vietnam had rendered everything else unreliable. Anne seemed to agree. We were enough in love that the world looked the same to both of us, and we felt like fugitives up there in the mountains, hiding out from the craziness of the other places we had lived. Our aim was to settle where we could live simply, cheaply, and deliberately. Having no desire to preach, we were not looking for Walden, only for plain and solid ground. And eight thousand feet high in the mountains of northern New Mexico, in a village tucked far out of sight of the highway, we thought we might have found it.

The old man was one of the first neighbors we met. He, his wife, and his oldest son, who spent most of the year herding sheep in Wyoming, lived next door to the house we initially rented. In his nearly eighty years the old man had been a farmer and rancher, a cook, a bootlegger, a miller, briefly a miner, and longest of all, for over fifty years, a sheepherder. For ten or fifteen years he had also been Democratic chairman for our village, El Valle, which the Board of Elections recognized as an independent precinct.

When we arrived, the precinct listed fifty-six registered voters. The old man quickly noted that we would increase the roster of Democrats by more than ten percent—if only he could recruit us to register with him. Not many days passed before he paid us a formal call—on party business. For the occasion he left at home his customary denims and rubber irrigation boots and wore instead a gray felt hat and a dark suit, shiny at the elbows, which was cut with a whimsy suggesting neither time nor fashion. He wore zip-up, tooled leather boots that were not just oiled but brightly shined, and the throat of his gold shirt was closed by a black bow tie, pre-tied from the store, its plastic hook and tabs barely concealed by the collar. Next to his leathery skin and Indian-nickel features, the Sunday suit seemed incongruously prim. It was plain that the man inside the polyester was as durable as a juniper stump.

Accompanying him were two aspiring Taos county officials. "This is Beatrice Sandoval," he said. "She is running for clerk. And this is José Silva, running for commissioner." He paused as we mumbled "pleased to meet you" and "same here." Then he stuck out a huge brown hand with fingers splayed at wild arthritic angles, and said with a hint of mockery, but of himself, the politicians, or us we could not be sure, "And this is me. Jacobo Romero. I am your neighbor."

Anglos who come to these mountains are always struck by the names. In a day you might pass Epimenio, Gomersindo, and Eremita on the road, while other neighbors like José and María, bearing names you've known all your life, stop to chat at the store. The name *Jacobo* had both qualities—it was familiar because of its English cognate yet wholly Span-

ish in the way it felt on the tongue: *ha-co-bo*. The village, too, was a combination of familiar and foreign. It was a small, poor, farming and ranching community much like thousands of isolated communities elsewhere, yet it could not have been mistaken for any other place. The valley which enclosed its green fields was once part of the Spanish and Mexican frontier. From the day of its founding to the present, El Valle, like sister villages in other valleys, lay so far from the main paths of the world that even the barbed wire in the fence gates seemed to creak in the old-fashioned, backwoods Spanish that was spoken there.

Jacobo began to call on us frequently, and we on him. He had a great curiosity about Alex's photography and passed many mornings in the darkroom at the back of our house, chatting with Alex and watching prints emerge from the developer. He liked to watch Anne too, partly for Anne's sake, for he had a fondness for the company of young women, particularly pretty ones, but partly also for the slow magic of the images she coaxed from her canvases. I, however, was at best a puzzle, more often a disappointment. Except when I left the village to labor as a carpenter, I spent my days hunched reclusively at a typewriter in the rear bedroom, pecking away, never very fast. No visible good came from what I did, which made my behavior harder to explain when I declined to pass a morning hour with coffee and talk.

"What do you want to do with all that typing?" he would ask, grimacing and making a show of poking his thick fingers at an imaginary keyboard. "Tap, tap, tap," he said, "you make too many words."

"Well, I'm writing a book."

"What about?"

"Maybe about these mountains. I don't know. I'm working it out."

"I see," he said. "Maybe when you finish you can decide what it is about." And he gave me a slow, tolerant nod, the same as he would give to any entry-level liar, then turned away saying, "*Bueno*, you are excused this morning, and Anne and Alex and Jacobo will drink all the coffee."

For the first year we lived in the village we had no dream of owning land there, and naively, no idea that anyone who owned land would be rash enough to sell it. But one day word reached us that a group of Anglo Santa Feans had come into ownership of forty acres at the bottom of the valley and wished to sell half. We hurried to strike a deal.

In an economic sense our ownership meant loss for Jacobo. Although he'd never owned the property, the fields we acquired were integral to the haying and grazing rotations that sustained his dozen cows and two horses. Previous owners, who rarely visited the land, had swapped him the use of it, rent free, in exchange for his maintaining the ditches and water rights.

After our purchase, Jacobo continued to manage the land the Santa Feans kept, which faced ours across the river. He called their field Los Americanos, and when he told his wife he was going to Los Americanos, she knew he would be gone for at least an hour, maybe several, for it was the farthest limit of the lands he managed and he would likely be obliged to rest in some sunny corner of pasture along the way.

No fence divided our land from Los Americanos. Only the river did, and we happily agreed to share with Jacobo the few acres of meadow that

lay on our side of the river. But as new landowners and aspiring farmers, we had other plans for the rest of our land. We aimed to grow hay in the big, fenced upper field, on our own.

If Jacobo regretted the loss of the field, he did not show it. He seemed to welcome us as active neighbors, as partners in common projects, and, in a way, as students. Clearly, we needed a teacher. None of us had irrigated, built a fence, or handled stock before. But we were lucky that Jacobo seemed to have a fondness, if not for us, then for the habit of instruction. Although he had more than forty grandchildren, none of them lived in the village, and it was his nature to seek out friendships and share what he knew.

Early on, he explained that while things might be done differently on other ditches, on ours, La Acequia Abajo, irrigation generally took place in several stages. The first began at six in the afternoon, when the previous user of the water released it, and the next irrigator's turn began. You first watered your vegetable garden, if you had one; then you set the water to run in the field for the night, and went home to bed. In the morning before breakfast you moved the water to another section of the field, and you came back and moved it again before lunch. If there was plenty of water and you spread it well, every corner of the field would have a good drink by six in the afternoon, when the turn of the next irrigator began.

That much seemed simple. Little else was so straightforward.

Reason suggests that if it is raining hard when the water comes to you, you might elect to leave irrigation in the charge of the heavens and to pass your turn. If it is snowing, which is not unusual at our elevation during the first weeks of the irrigation season, you will want to judge whether the soil of your field will be better moistened by the slow melting snow or by the ditch water that would wash the snow away. But if you are new to irrigation, as we were, you might surrender your own judgment and rely wholly upon the advice of an old, experienced neighbor like Jacobo.

We felt secure in doing so because other neighbors indicated by their off-hand compliments that Jacobo, of all the farmers in the village, was the most relentlessly conscientious. On the subject of irrigation his advice never varied. Regardless of rain, sleet, or snow, he instructed us always to spread the water, to irrigate even in a downpour, no matter if Noah's ark sailed into view. If we were crazy to obey him, or he was crazy to teach us as he did, we had no way to know. At least we could always see, as we squinted through the rain, that he too labored shovel in hand, several fence lines away, to soak his drenched fields with more water.

It rained so hard for the twenty-four hours before our first irrigation that the arroyo by the graveyard surged with runoff and springs burst from the gullies at the bottom of the hayfield. No matter. By mid-afternoon the clouds cleared and the sun reappeared, and at six we met Jacobo beside a muddy ditchbank to assist him in setting water for the night. In fact, he needed no help and it took him less than fifteen minutes to complete the task while we leaned on our shovels and watched him. The job done, we gave him a ride back to his house.

"What time do you want to move the water in the morning, Jacobo?"

"Maybe six thirty."

"Okay, we'll pick you up at six thirty."

"Fine. I see you then."

At five minutes to six we heard the rap of the old man's cane on our door. He had awakened early and was ready to work. He refused a cup of coffee but fidgeted in the kitchen, tapping the cane on the floor while we gathered boots and jackets. On the half mile truck ride to the land Anne, Jacobo, and I crowded into the cab while Alex rode in the back with the clattering shovels. Our dogs raced behind.

The illogic of irrigating land that was saturated from the previous day's downpour seemed more vexing in the chill of an uncoffeed dawn than it had the day before. Hoping he would not think I was questioning his judgment, I asked, "Jacobo, why do we irrigate even when there is plenty of rain?"

He placed a big hand on Anne's knee. "Because Anne," he said, pronouncing her name with a broad open vowel like the sound in the word es-pa-ña, "because Anne don't know when it will rain again, and you and me don't know as much as Anne."

As the graveyard came in view, we turned off the main road and jolted down a rutted track between low junipers that grew like green fists punched from the ground. At a line of taller, stately cedars marking the bank of the irrigation ditch, the road bent hard to the right, past the base of a gravelly hill. The truck swayed side to side, laboring in the mud. Fifty yards farther, the road ended at a broken down corral overgrown with chamisa and clematis. When I cut the engine, the sound of the ditch came to us like growling dogs. Alex climbed down stiffly from the truckbed. The hard ride and early hour had caused him, too, to question the need for watering a sodden field. As we crossed a plank bridge over the ditch and passed beneath the cedars to the field, he asked if it might not make sense to pass our turn at irrigation.

"Well, you don't want to give it up," Jacobo told him.

"Why not?"

"Maybe the *mayordomo* don't give it to you next time if you don't use it."

"Even if the *mayordomo* himself gives it up?"

"Maybe that *mayordomo* is a mean man. Maybe he could get a bad idea about you." Jacobo looked at Alex as though he might be getting a bad idea himself. Then he strode off. "Now we got to get going, and I go first."

He shambled along the top edge of the field, a cane in one hand and a short-handled shovel in the other, which he used like a cane, leaning heavily on both. He worked his arms as hard as his legs, so that he moved in a rolling, four-legged gait. We followed close behind in dull silence. He muttered at us over his shoulder, "If I fall down you got to pick me up. That's why I walk in front. If I walk behind maybe you don't see me and nobody pick me up. So I stay there, I donno."

Ahead of us the sun had just topped round-domed Trampas Peak and bathed a portion of the field—and now us—in its light. As yet it gave no warmth. We all wore knee-high rubber boots and jackets closed to the neck against the cold. Behind us the longer slopes of the hayfield showed a slight glaze where the ditch water had run all night. Now the old man intended to cut the flow of the water and redirect it to a skinny neck of pasture at the upstream end of the field. He would leave it there a few hours and no more.

"*Vamos a ver la presita*," he said.

He handed his cane to Anne and trudged up the ditchbank to the water gate that served that part of the field. The water gate—*la presita*—was a dam made from a massive log that lay athwart the ditch. Half of the center section of the log had been hewn out so that water might flow over it, and the ends of the log were buried in either bank. The nearer end, however, had been hollowed to form a side gate through which the water might be channeled to the field.

Jacobo fitted a gray pine board, its sides smooth from long use, in the guide slots of the log so that it stood where the log had been hewn. He tapped the board down with the shovel. The ditch water, backing against the board, seemed to pause for an instant and then burst loudly through the hollowed side gate toward the field. The ditch continued to fill against the board and in a moment shot a smooth and resonant curtain of water over the top of it. Jacobo pried the board higher for a moment and then tapped it part way down again, each change blending a new sound from the voices of the water. Finally the volume charging through the side gate suited him, and he turned and followed the water to the field.

Jacobo paused as the flow surged past him and topped the sides of the feeder ditch, spilling into the field. Near the water gate the feeder ditch, which he called a *regadera*, was at least a foot deep and almost as wide, but as it curved along the upper edge of the field, it tapered, obedient to years or shaping by Jacobo and others, to the merest depression no deeper than a cupped hand, and then disappeared altogether in the spring grass.

The water we were spreading belonged to the Río de las Trampas, the same stream that bathed the cottonwoods at the foot of our land. Translated, the name means River of the Traps, and, like most people, I had initially assumed the traps in question were beaver traps. The region, after all, once abounded with beaver and was a prime hunting ground in the early days of the Rocky Mountain fur trade. But it finally dawned on me, in the course of rummaging through libraries in Santa Fe and Albuquerque, that the river acquired its name long before a market for beaver existed, and long before Mountain Men or Spanish colonists were likely to have trapped them.

I asked Jacobo about the name. "Seems to me it could mean any kind of trap," he said. "They just always call the river by that name." And none of the other old-timers could shed more light than that, which rendered the name all the more enigmatic—it was the River of Traps for God-Knows-What. I found I liked it that way. I reasoned that a trap without quarry was the best-hidden, most subtle kind, the perfect snare. Look out, it seemed to say, you could be next.

A short distance downstream from El Valle, through the box canyon, the village of Las Trampas straddled the river. Trampas was the oldest Spanish village in the high mountains. As near as I could tell from the historical record, the people of Las Trampas, Jacobo's ancestors, probably began clearing and plowing land in El Valle within a decade or two of 1800. One of their first labors was to dig the ditch, or *acequia*, that served our land. They laid it out along the uphill edge of a string of meadows and pine flats, then sowed the land to wheat. The ditch began at a *presa* or head gate on the river a mile above our place, then contoured along the valley floor, capturing as much land within its arc as the slope of the terrain allowed. As the *acequia* curved along the tops of the fields, numerous *presitas* interrupted its course, and *regaderas* radiated from each like capillaries from an artery. At the bottom of our place, where the walls of the canyon sealed the valley off, the ditch debouched into the river, and gave its water back.

You had to admire those first settlers. There are sections of the ditch where the water runs without a sound, its surface flat as glass. Without benefit of transits or levels they laid the ditch out so that the water neither charged nor pooled. They eased it along, although the land was not easy, transforming the valley into a garden. But intellectual admiration is different from understanding through your bones. As time went on, I dug several score of post holes, numerous *regaderas*, and a few graves. I can testify that the stony soil of our valley does not yield easily to pick and shovel. But I have had all the help that hardware manufacturers can give. Compared to what those first settlers faced, I have been digging in beach sand. They had no iron, no steel. They made their tools from nothing more durable than fire-hardened wood. What was durable was their character. They had to be as tough and relentless as the builders of the pyramids.

Jacobo paused from his labors to reflect on the builders of the ditch. "I don't say they work like a dog," he said wiping his forehead with a blue bandanna, "because I never seen a dog do any work. But they work like a horse, maybe like five or ten horses, to dig all that and bring the water." He said he admired the way they laid out the path of the ditch, but their technique, in his opinion, held no mystery. "They dig a little, and they put a little water to see how it goes. Then they dig some more until it goes how they want. They don't worry where to put the ditch. They just let the water show them."

When he was a boy, Jacobo used to listen to the old-timers tell stories that harkened to the early days of settlement. Most of the time he paid attention, he said, but "never enough." In 1907, when he was ten and New Mexico was still a territory, the old folks he listened to could describe, firsthand, how life had been, living under the flag of Mexico. And the oldest of the old, those in their nineties when Jacobo was ten, would have begun their lives before the Mexican Republic was even formed, when the people of El Valle and every other New Mexican village were subjects of the Spanish Crown.

"Those *viejos* used to say the first land anybody used in El Valle was some *vegas* down by the *cañoncito*—more or less the land that belongs now to you. You have seen that trail in the *cañon*? They say they used to come that way from Trampas. Every day they come, and go back the same. They made a *molino* in the *cañon* where they could grind the grain to take back only flour and bran to Las Trampas. After a while, I guess they got tired of going back and forth, and they decided to make some houses here. That was how El Valle started."

Engraved on the bell of the El Valle church is the date 1850. By then, as a result of conquest, the village had been under the rule of the United States for four years.

Jacobo follows the water from the *acequia* to the *regadera*, and as he walks, he uses his shovel to chop notches in the side of the ditch, through which more water flows to the field. He also clears the ditch as he goes, flipping rafts of dead grass to the high side where they cannot obstruct the water's flow. Occasionally he stops to dig the channel deeper or to plug a leak with a clod of root-bound mud. "You see," he says, "if you don't want so much water to come out, you just take some of this *césped*, and put him in the way." And he slaps the clod into place with the flat of the shovel.

There is a stumpy-legged grace to his movements as he paces the ditch, shaping the soggy turf into contours that leak at just the right rate in just the right places. Each movement is exact and final, the shovel blade never touching the same earth twice. He is tuning the water, watching and listening to it like a technician attending his instruments, amplifying the flow here, muting it there, adjusting, repairing, and rearranging. In his hands the shovel seems as precise as a piano tuner's wrench.

It is plain that the shovel has been many hours in hardened hands. Its weathered shaft, gray and grained with age, is bound below the hand-forged handle and again at the throat with steel collars pitted by rust. The blade is sharply filed and bright with use, but where it should come to a point, it is scalloped instead, decades of use having bitten out the steel.

The old man strokes the last faint trace of the *regadera* with his shovel and turns to face us. He breathes heavily and leans on the shovel with both hands. "See?" he says, as though there is nothing in his short demonstration that warrants explanation. "You put the water out little by little until you have about this much at the end. Then you go back and look it over to be sure you got it right."

Again we face the sun, and its flat rays gleam on the spreading water. Clumps of orchard grass, taller and greener than the rest, rise above the shimmer, marking deposits of last fall's manure. The field appears shaggy, raw, yet with the water, strangely jeweled. Among the shrubs that grow along its edge, a few fall leaves still cling, yellow in the wild plums, rust in the sumac. To the right toward the river, magpies jeer from the bare limbs of the cottonwoods. Only the eastern peaks, distant and snowcapped, seem finished and well formed. Our ragged land, sodden and still drugged with winter, appears to be in molt. It cannot pass for pretty, but we know it has strength. We hope, uncertainly, that we do too. We are just beginning to understand how much we have to learn, how little we know.

Jacobo works his way back toward the ditch gate, against the path of the waters, seldom correcting his earlier adjustments but dividing the new generation of rivulets he has made into still tinier streams that spread separately through the grass. Again, his shovel is sure and deft, the movements small but exact. I marvel at the economy with which he works, and silently congratulate myself that I understand the purpose of each stroke—but only after it is made. The plan behind those strokes, the strategy of the field, remains a mystery. I cannot predict how much or how little water he will set loose at any point along the *regadera*, and not knowing that, realize I know nothing. It is the portioning of water to the different drifts and strikes of the slope that makes the difference between gullies and wholeness, between desert and hay. I watch him dumbly, like someone who understands a language when he hears it, but cannot speak a word. My only consolation is the expectation—and the hope—that Alex is no less confused than I.

Finally Alex asks the obvious and necessary question: "Jacobo, how do you decide to put a lot of water in this place and just a little water in that one?"

The old man pauses, leaning again on the shovel, and gestures downhill to vague places in the field, "Because that water will run together with this one and make too much where it passes the fence over there, and this water can be a lot because it is going by itself more or less to the bottom."

Jacobo's words seem more an incantation than an answer. I am relieved that Alex is also unsatisfied. He presses the question: "But from here, how do you know for sure what each water is going to do?"

"Well, you just got to learn, I guess. You got to let the water show you. You take your time, and sooner or later the water will show."

Jacobo resumes his labors, and we walk down the slope of the field to see if we can read the spreading waters. Our boots make a slapping sound on the sheet of water Jacobo has set loose. Flood waters from yesterday's storm have pushed up little mounds of twigs and straw, which we break apart. In one pile of flotsam we find the faded rose from the graveyard.

"Jacobo, one of the *difuntos* sent us a flower."

"Yah, you better save that. You going to need it for me when you take me to the *camposanto* to stay with those *difuntos*."

"Maybe this flower will wilt before you do."

"Maybe. You better save it and see."

He is finished for now. We stand beside the juniper where the water tumbles from the *acequia* and angles toward the field. Long ago the juniper was pruned to open a path to the ditch gate, and browsing cattle have kept it trimmed as neatly as a tree in an architect's diorama. Jacobo hangs his shovel on the stub of a branch and takes a tin of snuff from his breast pocket. The menthol-green label proclaims the brand is Copenhagen. Jacobo places a pinch behind his lip and says, "We'll come back in two hours and move the water."

The sun has dispersed the shadows where we stand. A towhee calls atop a willow, and a clutch of magpies squawk from a thicket of plums. The dew is warming. I can smell the humid odor of the sod.

The lowest branch of the juniper where Jacobo hung his shovel is about chin-high. I fasten the white rose to it, twisting the wire stem around the branch. Then, Jacobo leading, we head back to the truck.

2

Water Will Show

Without taking shovel in hand and making the attempt, one cannot appreciate the skill required to convert a volume of flowing water, one foot high and two feet wide, into an even sheet half an inch thick and an acre in size. Not that it takes any great skill to give a field a drink, as our efforts throughout that first summer proved. But after each effort, when we gave up the water at six o'clock, there remained large areas where the parched soil testified to our failure. We grew so used to bad results that we gave those places names: Texas, in the corner near the *cañoncito*, was our largest dry prairie, while the Jornada del Muerto, down from the first ditch gate, presented a strip of perfect wasteland. There was also dreaded Albuquerque, near the Jornada, whose gopher-mound subdivisions and tunnel interchanges drained precious water from the field.

Eventually we learned that similar microdeserts existed in the hayfields and pastures of other neighbors. But not, it seemed, in Jacobo's. His fields flourished because he had the eye to read the roll of the land, to let the water show him whether it would reach the dry spots or run together with other flows, gnawing gullies. But other village farmers could read the land as well. What set Jacobo apart was that he never "gave holiday" to the water—or to himself.

Jacobo slept alone in a room at the far end of his house. There was a lamp by the bed and a naked bulb overhead. The furnishings included a dresser, a wood stove, a narrow wrought iron bed, and a large freezer, stark and white, its compressor gently humming. The freezer, by far the most massive object in the room, held the year's supply of meat. Jacobo usually rose at dawn or a little before, dressed in denims, boots, and hat, then visited his *officina*, an outhouse perched beside the main trail to his fields, which he preferred to the indoor bathroom next to the kitchen, regardless of season.

From the office he followed a short trail through cottonwoods, past the household dump, to the top gate of his largest hayfield. If it were August, he might notice with pleasure that the orchard grass had headed out and the timothy had at last begun to flower. He might press on, following the top of the field, to the *regadera* where he'd let the water flow all night. He had no particular regard for the birds that sang noisily in the first light, and knew the names of only a few: the magpie or *urraca*, and the raven, which he called a crow. The songbirds flitting in the brush at the edge of the field drew none of his attention, nor did the dog that trotted at his heels. The dog belonged to Lalo, his son, who herded sheep in Wyoming, and it served some purpose as a watchdog but overall, in Jacobo's view, failed to earn its keep.

He found his scallop-bladed shovel hanging from the stub of a juniper branch, where he'd left it the night before, and set about moving the water. The business of this day, as of every other day in growing season, was irrigation. His farm, large by village standards, was served by three *surcos* on the Acequia Abajo, each *surco* being a full share or water right among the seventeen that existed on the ditch. He also irrigated from a small ditch on the far side of the river, which he alone controlled. It served both his land and Los Americanos. Except when drought required that water be closely rationed, Jacobo irrigated several fields at once, and always the pasture on the far side of the river.

Finished with the water in one field, he moved on to the next, surveying his animals as he went—the two horses in the orchard, where he could catch them easily, the dozen mother cows with calves, in two bunches, in the stony ground by the river.

There was one cow he particularly liked, black with a white face, that stood out from the red Herefords. She threw a strong calf each spring and took good care of it, giving plenty of milk. He liked to take time from irrigating just to watch her. Big-eyed, ruminating, she seemed to like watching him too. Sometimes she approached close enough for him to scratch her ears, and when he strode on to the next section of ditch, she followed like the dog.

The last ditch set, he gazed up the valley. The sun had climbed the length of a hand over the eastern peaks. It was time to go back to the house, where his wife would have readied coffee and breakfast. He hung his shovel in a tree and trudged homeward.

On the porch he removed his boots and went in.

"How are your cows, old man?" she asked.

"Still eating. Like cows." And he sat in his place at the formica table.

He was an easy man to cook for. He ate meat, chile, beans, eggs, bread, corn, and tortillas. He ate no salads, nor any green vegetable but chile. "I am not a cow," he said. "I don't eat weeds."

If a calf had been born in the night, he went to his room after breakfast and retrieved the pocket-sized notebook in which he recorded the event, noted the calf's markings and who its mother was and gave it a number. Then he pulled his boots on again and returned to the field.

If there was time for visiting, it came after he had moved the water a second time. Returning from the river he stopped at the orchard and bridled the ancient red horse. Jacobo was short and round, and the horse tall and thin. He had to saddle it at a road cut beside the garage, where he could stand high enough on the edge of the bank to heave the saddle up. The horse, broken to saddle and plow for more than thirty years, never failed to hold air against the cinch. Jacobo threaded the latigo through the cinch buckle, and holding the leather strap firmly in both hands, he turned his back to the horse and shoved his rump hard against its belly. He put his shoulder to the latigo and hauled forward with all his weight, nearly bending double, using his body as a lever. The horse groaned, released its air, and Jacobo tied off the cinch.

The round man on the gaunt horse was a fixture of the village. Eyes straight ahead, toothless mouth puckered, Jacobo sat deep in the saddle, whip in hand, while the red horse stepped carefully, sleepily down the road, as long-legged and deliberate as a praying mantis. Jacobo used an old-style mountain saddle with a high brass horn and a cantle that reached to the small of his back. Such a deep, cradling seat was dangerous if the horse fell and rolled on the rider but the support it gave was useful for steep mountain trails and long journeys. It was a saddle to live in, day after day, the way Jacobo had spent his younger years when he "followed the sheeps." For good or ill such saddles are scarce today, the standard of the western market being the safer flatland roping saddle, with a low cantle and pommel, that the rider can get in and out of quickly.

Jacobo and the horse were a partnership. They had been together since the horse was foaled on Jacobo's farm during or just after World War II, Jacobo couldn't exactly remember. Now, in their mutual old age, there was perhaps not another horse in New Mexico as slow and dependable, nor another rider for whom slowness and dependability were more important. Still, there was nothing of the pet or pet owner in either of them. The horse glared at Jacobo with the same hostile mistrust it glared at all the rest of the world. If the horse did not buck or bite, its restraint was due to hard lessons from the lash and, possibly, to a lack of surplus energy. For his part, Jacobo gave the horse no special consideration. He frequently left it hitched to a fence post, saddled and bridled, for half a day in the hot sun. Jacobo and the horse had a strictly business relationship. They did not socialize.

But thanks to the horse, Jacobo regularly visited friends from one end of the village to the other. "I don't need a newspaper," he said. "I just go *paseando*, *visitando*, and if somebody die in Taos, I hear about it before they write it down."

Jacobo's dependence on the horse was not altogether voluntary. Decades earlier he had tried to learn to drive, but without success. His older brother, Amador, had owned a car, Jacobo said, and patiently explained to him the operation of the vehicle. But when Jacobo got behind the wheel and pressed the starter, the roar of the engine echoed loudly between the walls of the house and garage and drove all thought from his mind. Still hoping to recall what Amador had taught him, Jacobo released the hand brake and stepped, too hard, on the accelerator. Instantly he realized he was lost. He could not remember the use of the steering wheel. The car careened down the road. Confused by the pedals, he stamped on both the brake and the accelerator together, and the car lunged and lurched even more erratically. A drainage ditch appeared ahead. He let go of everything. The car plunged in and slammed to a halt. End of lesson.

"Get someone else to teach you next time," said Amador, who drove the car back to the garage.

Jacobo walked.

I had sympathy for Jacobo's defeat by automobile. I too kept an uneasy peace with things mechanical, as did Alex and Anne. While we strove for self-reliance, cutting and hauling our firewood, killing and butchering our meat, we repeatedly met frustration with our vehicles. Other neighbors, far handier, routinely replaced bearings, rings, rods, whole engines. But Alex and I stretched our limits with tune-ups and valve adjustments. Jacobo visited one afternoon as I was extracting the end of a bolt I had managed to break off in my truck's engine block. I drilled a hole in the stub of the bolt, and started a bolt extractor into the hole. At the moment of maximum torque, when the broken stub should have begun to turn, my wrench slipped off the extractor and my hand flew into the hard square edge of the carburetor, gouging skin from two knuckles.

Jacobo repressed a smile while I cursed and kicked.

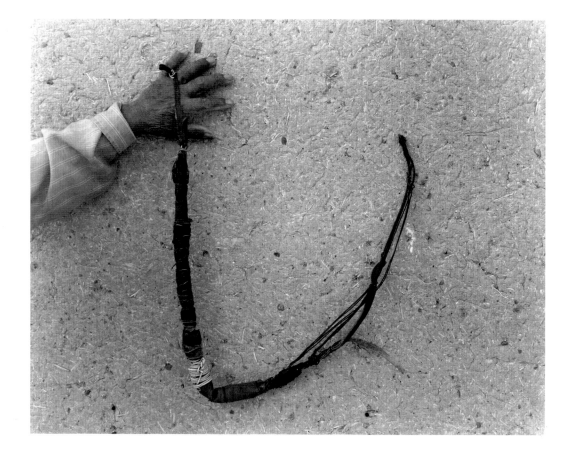

"Son of a bitchy bolt," he sympathized. "Engines *no valen nada*. They are no good."

Through clenched teeth I said, "Jacobo, I am no mechanic, only a carpenter. I have to work with wood."

"And I am a farmer. I have to work with dirt."

As with cars, Jacobo never mastered the use of chain saws, tractors, pumps or anything driven by gasoline. Until age slowed him, he relied exclusively on hand tools and horse-drawn equipment. He plowed our garden for us, next to the center gate at the top of the hayfield. He handled the team, and with difficulty I steered the single share plow, leaving furrows that were crooked but deep. The red horse, partnered with a muscle-bound roan, lunged hard to break the heavy sod, and Jacobo did not hesitate to sting either of them with the whip.

For handling the team and driving cattle he used a braided rawhide

whip eight or ten feet long. For riding, his "persuader" was a radically overgrown quirt, four feet or so in length, that also once was braided. But no more. The whip had unraveled with use, its leathers repeatedly breaking. In some instances Jacobo repaired the break by soaking the ends in water and joining them in a shrunken knot. Other times, he discarded the frayed leather and spliced in whatever was at hand—lamp cord, baling wire, shoe laces. He banded additional wire and patches of leather around the deteriorating handle and layered them over with thick wraps of electrical tape. In the end the thing looked less like a whip than the fetish of a crazed electrician.

The whip, like its owner, was humorous, even self-mocking. But no less than he, the thing was fundamentally practical, and when necessary, brutal. There was no place on the farm for sentimentality. A horse that was slow felt the lash. A barren cow was slaughtered. A dog that became a nuisance was killed, its body thrown in an arroyo. The net value of things was calculated not in dollars, possessions, or leisure, but in terms of food. All the irrigating, fence repair, haying, and tending of cattle led toward one goal: the production of meat. Meat was what the farm and the farmer existed for. To be sure, there was a reckoning in dollars. Jacobo was no fool about money, and still less was Liza, his wife, who often knew better than he what a steer would fetch at auction. But neither of them cared to separate net from gross, or to divide income by acres or acres by hours to know the return on capital and labor. Meat was meat, which was more than money. Meat was security, sustenance, the foundation of the household.

The work day ended when the sun went down, and the old man, in his eighth decade and hobbled with arthritis, plodded back to the house. He put his boots by the door, went to his room, and lay down. The last sound he heard before surrendering to sleep was the hum of the white freezer, full of meat.

That first summer Alex and I struggled to learn what the water would show us. Where Jacobo set the waters in fifteen or twenty minutes, we struggled for hours, digging and chopping the resistant earth. We were partners in the land but also competitors, each eager to show the other he was more the villager, more the man of the land, more the apt student of Jacobo. In a burst of industry, Alex dug a virtual canal to the Jornada del Muerto and, as the days went by, proudly pointed out to me how its grass grew green, if not tall.

Not to be outdone, I attacked Albuquerque with all my energy. I dug a trench by which I hoped to drown its denizens in their homes. I flooded the area, then plugged the burbling tunnels and prayed there'd be no gophers left to open them again. But always there were. After every onslaught, piles of dirt from fresh tunneling soon appeared. Albuquerque looked like hell while the Jornada blended back into the field. And Alex was just a trace too understanding the way he said, "Well, *you* can't win 'em all."

Until then I had admired the northern pocket gopher. Its burrowing helped aerate the soil of mountain meadows, a worthy contribution. In spring I used to marvel at the remains of the intricate tunnels it built beneath the winter snow. But in our field I came to see gophers as vermin, nothing more. Jacobo called them rats, pronouncing it RAT-*tes*, as though the plural were in Spanish. Alex and I called them rat-tes too.

During one attack on Albuquerque I looked up from the wet mess I was digging to see two magpies pecking at something the color of manure. The thing moved. I was too far away to make out what it was. A magpie pecked, then strutted past the soggy, living turd, and turning, pecked again. Suddenly the drenched thing stood up, mouth agape and tiny arms stretched outward like a boxer's. The magpie retreated while its partner stalked behind the thing and drove an awl-like bill into its neck. The magpies would have continued, but I cut short their fun. I ran to them, shovel high. With a full woodchopper's swing I brought down the flat of my shovel and merged the rodent with the soil. The gesture *was* excessive. Water spattered everywhere. I cringed to think there were gopher liquids in it. I looked around, relieved that neither Alex nor Jacobo was in sight, and brushed the droplets from my shirt.

Albuquerque eventually improved, but probably not from my efforts. Perhaps the coyotes that ranged our field at night, or our own dogs, which hunted relentlessly, finally limited the gopher population. Texas, however, half desert and half dustbowl, resisted us. It lay at the bottom of the sloping hayfield, where water should have reached it from our largest water gate.

That portion of the field posed two difficulties: its *regaderas* were riddled with gopher tunnels, and in contrast to the loamy clays in the rest of the field, the soil of Texas and environs was sandy and porous. The water leaked right through.

Working together, Alex and I attacked the gophers, as I had at Albuquerque, with shovels and still more water. As the grass grew and hid the tunnels, our aggressiveness increased. At a hardware store in Española I found a supply of cyanide gas cartridges abandoned on a back shelf. Their dusty wrappers said they were guaranteed to eradicate gophers and other ground-dwelling rodents. I should have realized that if the things really worked, there'd have been bins of them in the front of the store, and their labels would have at least postdated the Korean War. But at the time, they seemed a form of deliverance.

To Jacobo's amusement, Alex and I spent days dropping gas bombs down gopher holes, then scrambling to plug other holes where the gas leaked out. Unfortunately, only about half the bombs would light. The rest sputtered and fizzled. We tried to ignite them every way we could—with burning newspapers, charcoal, even a brazing torch. Jacobo's pleasure in watching us grew steadily. He included a stop at our field in his customary rounds so he could daily see what new foolishness we'd devised. Ultimately, Alex and I had to admit that the cyanide cartridges had no discernible effect on the gophers.

"Maybe you better go back to the shovel," Jacobo said, and dutifully we did.

Unlike Jacobo, who regularly flushed soggy gophers from their tunnels and whacked them dead, we logged few certain kills. But conditions improved, and perhaps we had the coyotes and the dogs to thank again.

The porous soil was a different matter. We had to overcome our fear of starting new gullies and learn to push huge volumes of water from the gate. We became increasingly macho in the way we dared each other to "blast" large flows along the crown of slope that was the only path to Texas. Our efforts escalated to the point, during one round of irrigation, that Alex pledged that when he set the evening water, he'd concentrate the entire contents of the ditch on Texas. It was my job to go out early the next morning and check how far the water had advanced. I did so with trepidation, for not only were the Texas soils thirstier, they were also more erodible, and I half expected to find that Alex's bravado had resulted in a gully.

I went down to the field soon after first light and found water gushing from the *presita*. A fair portion of it—but hardly all—was focused on the ridge that led to Texas, which remained dry, except for a dampened upper edge. It was clear that Alex had lost heart when he set the water the evening before. He had not made good his boast to "blast" Texas with all the water he could give it.

Now it was my turn to be bold. I told Alex he should have taken more of a chance and let the waters flow. I passed the rest of the day forcing still larger and larger amounts of water toward Texas and making barbed comments about lost opportunities, whenever Alex came in earshot. He was sheepish about his puny results, and we resolved, when we next irrigated, not to back away from an all-out, night-long inundation of miserable Texas.

Our chance came a week later. We focused every drop of water in the

ditch—enough to outgush a fire hydrant—on solitary Texas. Neither of us slept well that night, for what we did should have washed half our land to the Rio Grande. But in the morning when we went out to inspect the results, the surging waters had moistened no more than half of what was dry. The rest was only wet with dew.

The day was hot with no hint of rain in sight. We were in the prime of the growing season, and our nascent hay was wilting. We turned for advice to Jacobo, who dropped by the field in search of a missing cow—he said. He looked down upon us tolerantly from his high perch upon the red horse but offered nothing new by way of guidance. He admonished us again to "let the water show," and we thought we heard him hint, in the muted way he said it, that he'd given up on us, that he'd abandoned hope we might ever learn what he'd tried to teach.

But finally, as we puzzled through our problem, we did begin to glimpse an answer. The next time we irrigated, we again aimed the ditch at Texas and went to dinner. An hour after dark Alex and I drove down to the land. We parked at the corral and walked to the plank bridge over the ditch. The half moon was strong enough to cast a shadow from the cedars. A chorus of night insects whined.

The sound that was missing, however, was the sound of the ditch. At sundown, when we left it, it had brimmed with water. Now it was dry.

Alex drove back up the road to check if there were water at the headgate, while I, shovel in hand, began what promised to be a long walk up the *acequia* in search of water.

I found none in the ditch at the big field next to ours, which Tomás, our *mayordomo*, rented. And there was no water at the next field after that, which belonged to another neighbor. Jacobo's first field was also dry, and then I had to climb around the head of a small arroyo which the ditch spanned by flowing through, of all things, a missile launching tube. Several years earlier Tomás has procured five of them for the Acequia Abajo as part of some government program. The tube was an incongruous piece of equipment for a poor man's farm in a remote mountain range, but the olive cylinder, still bearing its serial number and hazard warnings, was stout, capacious, and long. The footing near the tube was slippery with leaves and lay in deep shadow. It was hard to move quietly. Farther along, a thicket of willows enveloped the ditch on either side, and I had to crawl on hands and knees.

At last I came to Jacobo's orchard, not far from his house, where the ditch growth opened up, and I could stand upright again. From not far ahead came the familiar gurgle of water running from a water gate. I went forward and found a board on edge across the ditch, held in place by several shovel bites of sod. The water, brimming against the board, gushed into a *regadera*. The orchard smelled damp and rich, heavy with the humidity of the soil. As silently as I could, I pulled out the board and laid it among the willows. I packed the clods into the mouth of the *regadera*, plugging it. The ditch water, freed, ran down the channel toward our land and the thirsty grasses of Texas.

Stealing water was a serious offense, punishable by fines, to say nothing of village censure. So far as we knew, the act of being stolen from was not a crime, but the censure, we were sure, would mark us for years. We said nothing to the *mayordomo*, and as I recall, Jacobo did not visit us the next day, nor for a few days after that. When he did come by again for talk and coffee, he said nothing of the taking of the water, and neither did we. Back then, we were still getting to know our neighbor—and letting the water show us.

Sunset Canto

June 21, the longest day. Tonight the stars will beam like headlights, and Scorpio will crawl along the ridge.

We'll drink and talk beneath the portal *and wait for heat lightning, red as Antares, to flash beyond the horizon.*

No car has passed for an hour. No chain saw has growled. The melt is over, and the river is low and quiet. Not the wind, but silence rolls in from afar.

There are near sounds: a blackbird in cattails by the river, swallows mewing on the power line. The sapsucker drums in the elm.

Whoosh.

Hear that?

Whoosh.

The nighthawks are up and wooing their mates with dives. They climb to the limit of sight, then plummet until—whoosh—they brake within feet of the ground. Each night at dusk they make this dance, plunging in and out of sunset.

The final light blazes on the blind man's house, last house in the valley. It gleams on the transformers and the signs for Quality Oil and Chevron.

It lingers on the peaks, bare islands in a sea that laps the edges of our fields, waiting to reclaim them.

Comes the old man on his canes. Huffs as he climbs from the road. "Son of a bitchy bull, gone all the way to Orlando. Broke the fence again. Maybe tomorrow you help me bring her." *The road is dusty, dry. Yes he'll take a beer.*

Montoyita, how is he?

"Fine. Fine."

And Juan de Dios?

"Todavía the same. Weak to walk. Fine to sit."

Silence, and we watch the valley. Sound of sipping and swallowing. Sound of bottles put down on the rough cement stoop. Sound of circling nighthawks, calling eep, eep, *as they hunt and swoop.*

The chamisa darkens by the road. The light of the blind man's house goes out. Now a coyote starts up. Now a car.

"All right, thank you. I got to go while I can see. That vieja *is waiting." He edges down the bank, weight on the canes, loose dirt sliding before him. He reaches the bottom, stamps his boots clean.*

See you tomorrow.

"You see me tomorrow, yes. If I don't die and you don't go blind."

He raises high the righthand cane, a salute without looking, and shuffles down the road.

Comes now the light of the moon and the red eye of Antares, staring from the dark above the llano. *Somewhere by the river an owl begins to hoot.*

3

The Right Place

It is September 1972, and Alex and I are in Peñasco staring out the big glass windows of Victor's Drive-In, at the uncrowded west end of town. Victor's is the only place in Peñasco where everything is new: the big windows, the formica tables, stainless steel counters, and shiny kitchen equipment. We are twenty-two and cocky. The memory of college is slightly more than a year old for Alex, mere months for me. The cheeseburgers we eat taste reassuringly like the cheeseburgers that nourished us weeks earlier in other hamburger sheds far away. We are as new and anomalous in this weathered town as Victor's glass and chrome.

We share a table with Lucien, Marshall, and Ruth, three commune hippies we met as we waited for food. They say they live without running water or electricity in a place so remote they have to pack in their goods by foot or horse. They have gentle smiles. They say they are building houses, plowing fields. They live together as one family with a half-dozen others and rarely come to town. We don't get the feeling, as they tell us this, that they are trying to impress us.

We explain to Lucien, who does the talking for the three, that we are looking for a place to live. He wears a wispy black beard and a ponytail; one of his front teeth is missing. "We're working on a place too," he says. "It took us three years to get our land together." The suggestion is there. We should relax, be patient. A couple of years, and we can have a place too.

Dirty-faced Marshall, who is younger even than we, has not paused to acknowledge our presence. He devours his burger and fries as though the food might vanish. Ruth, next to him, is skinny and nervous and seems too delicate to bear the mud and drudgery of life in a cowpath commune.

She stares at her food glassily and pokes it with a fork. While Lucien speaks, I find myself looking at Ruth. She is very pretty. I wonder what I might say to her, if we had a chance to talk alone. Everything I think of sounds too square, too conventional.

We ask Lucien if he knows anyone we might ask about a place, and he reflects for a moment. Perhaps we sound overeager, a little pushy. When he speaks, he tries to slow us down. "I can't say how it will be for you because everybody's trip works out different," he says, "but you'll find a place if you're meant to."

Under the circumstances, his advice did not seem trite. We nod. Maybe he's right. Maybe things will take care of themselves. We tell him we'll probably have a look around Taos later that day. "You ought to stay away from there," he warns. "In Taos it's tough to get your scene together. Too many energy leaks." He smiles, and the black hole in his teeth flashes like a wink. We smile back, outwardly mulling and approving the idea of energy leaks. Privately I'm caught between admiration for this new-age Daniel Boone and skepticism that his cosmic poise derives from fried brain cells. Lucien gestures toward the plate-glass window and beyond to the pot-holed road and rusty-roofed barns of Peñasco. "You might try Ellie Cordova down in Rodarte. She could know of a place." We thank him and say goodbye.

As we leave, he tells us, "Watch out for the leaks. There are some here too."

We say we'll try. It can't hurt.

Ruth waves goodbye with a flick of her hand and then fights to repress a fit of giggles. Marshall ignores us and, while Ruth is turned around, scrapes french fries from her plate to his.

In Alex's Volkswagen, we drive through Peñasco, Alex at the wheel. I've known him only a few days and find him, at times, painfully shy. At the outset, I had the impression he was pudgy, slightly overweight. Now I am realizing he isn't fat, but he is so unassertive his edges seem soft. He seems most comfortable when he isn't obliged to talk, like now when he's driving, or anytime he has a camera in his hands.

Alex speeds through Peñasco, laughing and veering slightly side to side, pretending to dodge energy leaks. It's a good joke, but scarcely masks our shaken confidence. Our talk with Lucien reminds us how foreign the mountain world is. It will be easy to make mistakes.

We drive past an empty adobe warehouse and an abandoned dance hall;

we pass an Exxon station, the post office, a bar with a sagging roof called Tom's Place, and the enormous Roybal's Garage, which proclaims its name in peeling green letters on a white two-story facade. We drive by the Rainbow grocery store, which has a half-dozen motel rooms in back, and then past another bar, this one called El Norteño, which I have to think about to understand its name. Then I get it. We are in the Southwest only from an Anglo point of view. The people who settled Peñasco came from the south, from Mexico, and before that, New Spain. These mountains were the northern frontier, the home of northerners, *norteños*.

We pass a dozen cement-plastered houses with geraniums in their windows, and we marvel that the houses should crowd the road so tightly in a land where space seems so cheap, so limitless. We pass the Cotton Butane and more gas pumps and a cafe that's closed and a house with hollyhocks so thick around it, it seems to be hedged. We pass a long row of abandoned buildings and more buildings that aren't abandoned but should be; we pass the glass and cinderblock box of Owen's Grocery and Hardware Store, and then the sheet-metal quonset hut of Sahd's General Store. We turn off the main highway, taking the road to Rodarte and Llano de San Juan, a road that also leads, we note with some excitement, toward the high peaks.

As one village gives way to the next, the houses recede from the road, surrendering space to small hayfields and pastures where dull-eyed cows and roman-nosed horses graze. We pass a herd of thirty or forty scruffy sheep. Several houses, as we approach Rodarte, bear flagstone facings as orange as a hunter's jacket and outlandishly carved porch posts that have been varnished to a high shine. But most are simple, weather-beaten adobes, many with old cars abandoned in the yard, the hulks submerged in weeds or propped up on blocks, rims rusting. A bay horse lifts its head as we go by. Nothing and no one else is stirring.

It takes us an hour or more to find Ellie Cordova, who greets us cheerfully and then wrings her hands as she apologizes for not being able to think of a single good prospect. "*Boy*, I jes don't know of anything," she tells us, and she smiles and shakes her head. It was only later, when we were back in the car, that I began to wonder if she had considered us hippies. We didn't think of ourselves that way. Our hair was long, but we had jobs. Perhaps if we had told her that, she might have thought a little harder about the rentals that she knew.

We didn't make the same mistake with R. E. "Dick" Straycher, a realtor in Taos. Straycher's pseudo-log-cabin office on the south side of town boasted a sign that said "Specialist in Mountain Property." He sounded like the man for us.

Straycher's place smelled heavily of gun oil. An open box of Hoppes gun-cleaning pads lay on the coffee table beside copies of *Sports Illustrated* and *Field and Stream*. As we entered, Straycher placed an expensively tooled rifle in a gun rack that also held a pair of shotguns. Several safari pictures of defunct leopards and rhinos decorated the wall behind his desk. He invited us to sit on a red leather sofa and faced us from behind an oaken desk the size of a ball field.

We explained our situation. We were research assistants for a Harvard psychiatrist named Robert Coles, who was writing a book on Chicano and Indian children and their families. Alex needed a place to live where he could also set up a darkroom. I simply needed a place to live and write. We told Straycher that our work would go best if we lived in one of the older mountain villages, and we asked him which village he'd recommend and how we might find a place to rent.

Straycher stretched manfully in his chair and touched his hand to his forehead as though we had caused him pain. "Don't kid yourselves," he said. "Stay out of there. You go live up there and you'll get your ass peeled."

What? Did we hear him right?

"Any Anglo who goes up there," Straycher continued, "is just looking for trouble."

"Look," I said, "we know there's bad blood between the hippies and a lot of Chicanos but there are plenty of other Anglos—schoolteachers and doctors—who work up there and get along pretty well."

Straycher stared down at me as he might at a kindergarten child. He leaned forward, chair creaking loudly. "Just remember what I told you: if you go up to live there in Truchas, Peñasco, or any of those goddamned places, sooner or later you're going to get your ass peeled." The last phrase seemed to give him so much pleasure that he said it again, "Those locals will peel your ass."

We left Straycher's office in a fine state of rage and scarcely talked of anything else through the rest of the day and evening. If we had any doubts about whether to live in the mountains, Straycher's arrogance cured us of them. We'd find the right village on our own.

As it turned out, getting our asses peeled was purely elective—and Alex elected not to. He managed to rent a small house in Peñasco near the post office and set to work. His method was outwardly simple. Day after day, he drove the back roads of the mountains, hunting photographs. He'd arrive in a village, sometimes with an introduction, sometimes without, then meet people, get himself invited into their homes, take pictures, and leave with promises to return. He did return, too, a week or two later, with prints he gave away of the photographs he'd taken and with time to visit some more, the camera always ready as the visit unfolded. He seemed to me fearless in the way he entered those villages, those houses, those lives, but one thing didn't fit.

I couldn't understand how he could be at once so intrepid and still so quiet, almost withdrawn. A friend who ran a cafe where we frequently ate asked me, "What's the matter with Alex, doesn't he have anything to say?"

I said, "He's just not pushy, he's very laid back." My friend, who was talkative and liked others to be the same, said Alex had better watch out. "If he gets any more laid back, rigor mortis will set in!"

In the villages, if not in the cafes, most people were drawn to Alex, and the extreme quiet was part of his attraction. Being genuinely interested—but not in talking—he listened well; one felt his curiosity but sensed it was always in check, restrained by his gentle, Georgia-bred deference. Alex grew up in Atlanta, and the quiet manners he learned there served him well. Usually he was content to be part of the background, undemanding, unthreatening, happy to be there, the camera also in the background, its shutter sometimes clicking. I remember how jealous I was when he told me that a fellow he'd just met from Picuris Pueblo had invited him to celebrate Thanksgiving, Indian-style. They were going somewhere out on the Navajo Reservation, to the home of the Picuris man's wife's family. Alex told me of his plans for Thanksgiving-in-a-hogan in the most casual way, as though it were the kind of thing anybody might expect to do. He was lucky, I told him. And he was also, it seemed to me, very brave to let down his guard so much with total strangers.

His work through the year went well, culminating in the publication of a book called *The Old Ones of New Mexico* with our employer, Robert Coles. It was a portrait—and thanks to the way Coles brought in the voices of others—a self-portrait of a generation of villagers who had grown up near the turn of the century in conditions of pioneer hardship and self-sufficiency. Jacobo and Liza Romero didn't figure in it—Alex hadn't met them yet, but in later editions they would.

While Alex was being brave, I was mainly being brazen.

I rented a house in Truchas on the main road. One of the first visits I made was to Clarence Pacheco's bar. I introduced myself to Clarence, and over a Schlitz we talked about how it was to be a stranger in a new place. Clarence said he knew the feeling; he'd been stationed in Alaska during the war. He reached behind him and tapped the big .44 that hung in a holster between the peppermint gins and some bottles of vile pink stuff.

"I can remember how it was to be a stranger," he said. "It is not easy. So you can come to my bar. I will protect you."

At first I did not understand his offer. I was too new to Truchas and too ignorant of life there. Days later I realized that Clarence was pledging to intervene in order to keep my ass from being peeled in his bar, which would otherwise have been a fair certainty. Just the same, when I learned how rough the bar tended to be, I stayed away on weekends and didn't push my luck. Clarence and his .44, however, could not also protect me from myself.

I paid attention that year to everything except my job. I plunged into a disastrous love affair with a tall beauty from North Carolina who played an exceptional game of pool. We regularly called the corner pocket at Mel Patch's Lounge in Española. We indulged ourselves in bank shots, late beers, and dramatic arguments. Ending the affair became a full-time job that lasted months, and it didn't end well. Nor did other endeavors. The few pages that passed through my typewriter went straight to the trash. I managed to step in the middle of two neighbors' feud and got beat up for my pains. Coles should have fired me, but instead the grant ran out.

When twelve months had passed, I built a camper for the back of my truck, loaded it with everything I owned, and headed west with no particular intention of returning to New Mexico.

The primary focus of Alex's work soon shifted far from the Southwest, to Eskimo communities in remotest Alaska, but he continued to keep the house in Peñasco. It was his base, and adequate for that, but not his home.

He hoped for more. As he continued to explore the mountain villages, he assessed each as a place to live, perhaps permanently. One village in particular caught his eye. It lay not far from Peñasco in a broad valley some distance from the paved highway. He was attracted to its open pastures, to the quiet of its tan, rockstrewn road, to the forested ridges that enclosed the village but did not squeeze it too tightly.

A lively river snaked down the bottom of the valley beneath an arch of cottonwoods. Back from the river spread the fields and the orchards, sloping upward to pastel houses, pink, ocher, and green. One of these houses, blue and white, overlooked the road from the shoulder of a hill.

The plaster was cracked and the cement of the porch crumbled easily. Behind the house lay a scatter of outbuildings—a root cellar with its roof caved in, a log chicken house, empty for years, a weathered tool shed whose plank door slammed in the wind, and several barns enclosed by a wire corral.

The place was vacant when he first saw it, and once or twice he climbed the steep drive and looked in the windows. The beams sagged and the floors and other woodwork were crude, but with each inspection he became more convinced that it was the right place to live.

He was attracted to the house for all the reasons he was attracted to northern New Mexico. It had a hard-used, simple elegance. It was of the people, of the place. By living there, he would enter that world more deeply, which could only help him as a photographer, as a person. So much of making pictures, or anything else, was a question of luck. You had to be in the right place at the right time. A house like that could tilt the odds in your favor.

Alex contacted the owners; they agreed to rent it to him. He built a darkroom in the back and refitted the bathroom and kitchen. Before he left for Alaska on a long trip, he called or was called by me, I can't remember which. I was working in San Francisco, the solitary straight man in a gay building company that restored Victorian townhouses. I said I'd dropped my hammer from the scaffold one time too many. I had to get out. I was going to write a book. I'd been saving for it, now was the time.

He said, "Come on."

I said, "I'm not alone now. Anne is an artist; she wants to paint in New Mexico."

He said, "No problem, there's plenty of room. I'll be in Alaska but the house will be unlocked."

I said, "Thanks, we'll just stay a couple of weeks, while we find a place in Santa Fe."

"Stay as long as you like."

4

Diamante

Journal entries:

May 7, 1975. El Valle.
Cows bellow like last week's foghorns. Elm by porch just budding. Well house, in orchard below the road, home to three small green snakes, one of them dead. Pump took priming, but works. House has no door or window casings, only jambs; no plumb corners; floors are all levels, with open seams between boards where dust drifts down; everything is stick style and homemade, even the ceiling beams are just trees peeled of bark and laid up atop walls; here and there the adobe masonry appears to swell slightly, as with breath. Hiss of the gas heater, blackbird in the bush.

May 10, 1975.
El Valle numbers are listed in the Truchas section of the phone book along with two other villages, including Las Trampas. Entire entry fits on one page. Under Fire (to report a Fire): 11 listings. Under Truchas, Village of, Fire Department: same 11. Also 2 stores, 1 school, 1 clinic, 1 community center, 1 Help Ctr. Final score: Spanish names 50, Anglo names 4, institutions 6, fire 22.

May 20, 1975.
Old man on horse very curious about us. Wants to know if we will register as Democrats or Republicans, where we come from, what we do, how come we work at night, if we work at night. Lives one house down the road. Must have seen the light. Short fellow, used to be strong; sneakers,

jeans, work shirt with button missing and bottom of breast pocket worn through from snuff tin that rides there: Copenhagen brand, with menthol.

June 11, 1975.

Many cars at Romero house. The old man's 78th birthday, according to Anne via Tomás, our other neighbor. Children from out of town. Found his red horse, saddled, grazing outside our kitchen window, near cesspool. Wire is down, several holes in the ground where cesspool timbers rotted and dirt falls through to the pit; horse could stumble in. Tallest, reddest, oldest horse I ever saw. I shooed it back toward their barns.

June 20, 1975.

Jacobo comes to visit, riding the red horse. Short man, tall horse, needs a stump or cutbank to mount. Turns the horse loose—to eat our "weeds," pronounced with two syllables: WEE-*des*. I tell him about the cesspool.

He says, "Let 'em fall in if he don't know better."

Does the horse have a name?

"No need for a name. I know which one he is."

How old is he?

"Thirty, maybe forty years. Was foaled sometime in the forties. Wartime, I think."

And after thirty years no name?

"No name. He don't give me a name neither, I think."

July 7, 1975.

From Jacobo: He was born in Diamante, five miles by road up the canyon and a thousand feet higher than El Valle. Used to be five families living there. They called it Diamante because of the deposit of white clay at the edge of the natural meadow: soil bright as diamonds, something like that. Children were shoeless, nearly year round—at 9,000 ft. Family was large, now only one sister in Iowa left. Meat, meat, meat, he says. Pig, steer, goat, sheep, chicken, "Mama say, 'Get me some fish,' and quick in fifteen minutes we come back from the river with plenty." The dogs ran deer from the north side of the canyon into deep drifts on the south, where his father or older brother finished them off. In winter his father would drive three horses abreast through snow to break trail for goats;

then cut down a tree, usually *pino real*, douglas fir. Goats eat the foliage; also wood provided and more pasture cleared. After a few days, branches bare, go cut another. . . .

The July 7 entry is a long one, the first of many drawing on Jacobo's recollections. It is faithful to the facts he shared but cannot capture the manner of his storytelling: the slight, hypnotic gestures of his enormous hands, the solemn, mask-like face breaking into a grin, the gleam in his eye when he sensed your disbelief or squeamishness and then bore in, teasing you, with outrageous, repugnant details.

"No, I never do like to eat bear. Was a time, I was a boy, no more than so high, my uncle shot a bear and brought him to the house. He hung that bear on the side of the barn and begin to skin him. I was watching. Pretty soon I can see that bear is a sow—a woman. And my uncle skin the belly and the chest so you see the flesh without the hide and you see the *tetas*, and without the hide, they look like the breasts of a woman. And that bear got hands like hands and feet like feet, and my uncle cut the head off with the hide, so the bear is hanging upside down, but it don't look like a bear no more. It look like something else, something like maybe a person. Because it got *tetas*. *Just Like a Woman Breasts*!" He rolls his head, tongue lolling, and spreads his arms as though crucified and dead. A moment passes. He pretends to revive. Peers out through groggy eyes and musters a confessional tone: "So, no. That's *no bueno*. I cannot eat that flesh, not that looks like a woman, with hands and feet and breasts. I cannot eat the flesh of a bear."

It was luck, pure and simple, that put us in the house next to Jacobo's. The house, in fact, had been built by his late brother, Amador, and was known by Amador's nickname: we lived in Moi's house.

It was lucky for us to be near such a character, lucky that he extended his friendship, and lucky, not least, that he liked to speak English. Not many of his generation spoke it as well as he, and we, sad to say, were utterly incompetent in Spanish, to say nothing of mastering the brand of *español*, heavy with archaisms and ridden with contractions, that was spoken in the mountains.

The English Jacobo used broke every rule of grammar and invented some rules of its own. One of his most confusing habits was to reverse the gender of third person pronouns. In Jacobo's stories *he* commonly became

she and *her* became *his* so that you never quite knew if the horse he spoke of belonged to a woman who had a gelding or a man who kept a mare. The matter was rendered more difficult by the fact that the reversal of genders was inconsistent. Cows were nearly always she, but mares, bitches, and women frequently were he, and inanimate things like horseshoes, cars, and fence posts might take on either gender, or both.

Jacobo was joined in this habit by other elders in the village, which made us wonder if an errant schoolteacher years earlier might not have started things on the wrong foot. But when we met old folks from other villages, who also confused genders, we realized there must have been a legion of misinformed teachers, or none at all.

Jacobo's formal education began late and passed quickly. Diamante lay at the limit of the habitable earth. It was little more than a high cold

widening of the river canyon, long since abandoned, where a few families lacking land elsewhere eked out a tenuous existence. Only one man among its hardy pioneers could read and owned a book. Sometimes he brought the children together and tried to teach them the alphabet. Mostly the children ran wild.

Jacobo was nine, maybe ten, when he first attended school. His experience with instruction that year was brief. The one-room schoolhouse in El Valle was in session only the three or so coldest months of winter when farm work came to a standstill and the children were not needed at home, day by day, as workers. On Sunday evenings his father drove him down from Diamante, a cold slow ride in the buckboard, and left him with relatives, returning to fetch him home the following Friday. The education was free but Jacobo and the other children still owed a kind of tuition.

Each day they walked to school with a stick of firewood under their arms to stoke the potbelly stove that warmed the room where they fidgeted through their lessons.

"The teacher," he said, "try to make us read and write in Spanish, but we don't care too much for that. We just play, play, play." One game he remembered, looking back from his old age, was to take slender sticks in either hand and hold them as imaginary forelegs. Then, bounding down the road, the child Jacobo pretended he was a deer. It was a favorite memory of the old man who hobbled on canes.

Eventually Jacobo learned English in the sheep camps of Utah and Wyoming. Although he may have failed to absorb some of its grammar, he had a gift of expression, and his use of the language was crisp, sharp-edged, even poetic:

> *Was a man had a dog to herd the cows. She tell 'em, "bite the cows, bite 'em," and that dog sure bite the ankles, move the cows to milking or back to pasture, wherever the man want them to go. Then the dog die and the man don't get another. But the man still go behind the cows and say, same way she used to say to the dog, "bite the cows, bite 'em." And those cows sure step along pretty good, just like the dog was there.*

The notes I wrote of his stories were never as detailed as I would later wish, for my attention was elsewhere—on the book I was trying to write. It was conceived modestly, if ambiguously, as a natural history and trail guide to the wild, higher reaches of the mountains, lands generally known as the Pecos Wilderness. As I proceeded, the project grew—grew out of control, I thought, and it filled me with anxieties about money and skill and failure. Next to those concerns, the stories of an old man who had long lived in the shadow of the mountains, but who scarcely knew their inner fastness, seemed peripheral, distracting.

But the book kept moving in his direction. I started out writing only about the land, its geology and ecology, all safe subjects in my view because they avoided the complexities of human affairs. But before long I discovered that the trails of natural history led also to villages and towns. There were people in the mountain landscape whom I could not ignore. They had used the land and ultimately altered it. Even more interesting

was the question of how the land had altered them, how natural history had shaped the history of cultures.

I did not expand the scope of the book in order to include Jacobo's stories, but if I'd been smarter I would have, and I'd have saved time. His stories eventually found their way into the manuscript because finally I realized that they cut to the heart of the tale I wished to tell. It was humbling for me as an aspiring scholar to plunge repeatedly into archive collections or the dusty back stacks of libraries, there to find that the kernel of understanding I sought was already with me, carried unnoticed like a burr on my clothing, in a story learned from Jacobo.

When I researched Spanish settlement of the region, for instance, I read in a carefully footnoted article that a village, outgrowing its resources, typically spawned another in a process called "hiving off." Immediately upon encountering the term I realized that Jacobo had already described the process to me in his account of how people from Las Trampas cleared land and farmed in El Valle, eventually to build houses and stay there. Later their children and grandchildren expanded in like manner up the river to Diamante, where Jacobo was born.

When I came to the story of the Las Trampas Land Grant, which was the legal instrument that initiated settlement of the area, I was confident the libraries and archives held all I needed to know. The records showed that the governor of the royal Spanish colony of New Mexico made the grant in 1751 to a band of otherwise landless peasants who represented a drain on the meager resources of Santa Fe. Among the governor's motives was the desire to throw a living and soon-to-be-bleeding human obstacle in the path of the Comanches, under whose raids the frontiers of the colony were crumbling.

Somehow the settlers of Las Trampas survived, and it is a wonder they did in view of their government's chronic inability to defend its citizens. The government was poor and inept, its people poorer but staunch and resilient. The people who settled the place called *The Traps* must have appreciated the irony of the name. They faced the Comanches' matchlock muskets without guns of their own, possessing only lances and bows and arrows. No less daunting was the short growing season and capricious weather of their mountain environment, which they battled without so much as a scrap of iron to harden the points of their heavy wooden plows. But they built their *acequias*, their fortified plaza, and their graceful church, and they labored, suffered, fought, and survived. Against such odds, the fact of their survival—and that of similar communities throughout the colony—marks the high point of sheer doggedness in the European settlement of North America. Theirs is an astounding, if unheralded, achievement. And perhaps unique in the history of the continent, the descendants of those first pioneers still live on the exact land their ancestors defended.

I was especially interested in an aspect of the land grant story that no one at that time had pieced together. It was the story of how the grant, which Anglo surveyors ultimately measured to include 28,131.66 acres, became alienated from the descendants of its original recipients. The passive phrase, *became alienated*, just about sums up what happened, for

virtually all the inhabitants of the grant remained ignorant—literally for decades—of the series of legal maneuverings by Anglo speculators and their Hispanic allies that finally, in the early years of this century, separated them from their patrimony—and from the resource base of forest and rangeland that for generations had sustained their communities.

The information I sought lay buried in reams of legal documents, but no sooner had I begun to sift the archives than I encountered the name Narciso Romero among those who had belatedly and for the most part vainly defended the villagers' ownership of the grant against the speculators. It turned out that Narciso Romero was Jacobo's father, and from Jacobo I learned a side of the story that the documents did not tell. It was the side that the villagers knew. It told how they finally filed suit to recover the entire grant—or thought they did, but in fact didn't. All their lawyer demanded in the action he brought was restoration of the villagers' ownership of the houses in which they dwelled and the fields they cultivated. Speculators had gained title to the land grant commons more than ten years earlier, without the villagers even knowing it. Thus they won a battle but lost the war, for although they regained title to their house plots and irrigated fields, they never understood how the balance of the grant—some 21,000 acres—was taken irrevocably from them.

The pattern of discovery persisted in other areas. Jacobo's account of breaking his leg when he was a boy—it was crushed beneath a wagon wheel, and his father set it in a homemade cast of cardboard—made real for me the severe isolation from outside help the villagers had known. Jacobo also told the story of how his brother, trailing an errant cow, discovered lakes at the foot of the high peaks. Narciso Romero disbelieved the boy, and set out to see for himself. Followed by a few of the older children, he clambered all the next day up the steep, choked canyon of the Río Trampas, where no one else, he thought, had gone before him. He followed game trails, climbed over deadfalls, and picked his way across boulders slick with moss and ice. He pressed ever upward to where the trees grew stunted and the wind growled. There the land became level, then bowl-like, and at last Narciso broke from the trees into an open expanse, as big as a rich man's farm, which was bounded by rubble-sided cliffs that reached to the clouds. There, in the center of the opening, he beheld a pair of emerald pools, deep and broad, with wind riffling their surface.

In actual fact, the Trampas Lakes had by then been "discovered" by other travelers, but that was of no great relevance to the pioneers of Diamante. The landscape in those days was fresh; the only maps the Romeros consulted were in their memories, and certain canyons and ridges remained uncharted and unknown. For me, Jacobo's story expressed how the *terra incognita* of the mountains seemed, in those days, a living thing, how the land, from the perspective of those who struggled in its grasp, was always dominant.

Later, when I sought to understand how the region—and indeed the entire West—was stripped of its best timber and grazed half to death, I again drew on Jacobo's recollections. It pleased him to recall his boyhood days when cattle ranged freely to the head of every canyon and he and other children, day after day, herded bands of sheep and goats over the piñon-studded hills. As he matured, he also worked as a logger, like every other able-bodied man in his family and village. He and his neighbors cut and squared by hand many of the ties that double-tracked the Atchison Topeka and Santa Fe across the Southwest. The dimes and quarters they received for their timbers helped feed a long-desired, if short-lived, prosperity in the village world, even as the mountains were denuded. Though the damage from heavy logging and grazing was enormous, it was impossible to think of Jacobo and the hardy souls who worked beside him in any negative light.

I next came to the story of the Forest Service, which acquired many of the old grants, the Trampas grant among them, from the scoundrels who had snatched them from the villagers. La Floresta, as the Forest Service became known, imposed stiff restrictions on the villagers' use of the land, on grazing seasons and herd limits, intending to restore health to the forests and rangelands, but often pursuing that intention in callous and bullying ways. Jacobo sometimes reminisced, without apparent bitterness, about the good old days before the rangers came, when "everything was free, and we paid for nothing, the fish and the deer, the grass wherever our animals could find it, wood for fuel and timber for building."

Everything was free, he said, except the few things the family bought with its little hoard of cash: sugar, salt, baking powder, sometimes but not often flour. There was a log grist mill at Diamante, powered by the river, where they ground the wheat they grew. It was a variety of wheat particular to high, cold environments, but no one has grown it in the region for decades. The cash economy gradually replaced that home-grown staple with a consumer necessity—wheat from the Great Plains.

When times were good and there was extra cash on hand, the family purchased manufactured hardware, harness, and farm tools from one of several general stores in Peñasco. Increasingly, as the years passed, they also bought ready-made shoes and even clothes, although gunny sack dresses were long considered adequate for the littlest ones. They were the only clothes Jacobo wore for the first four years of his life.

The women did the cooking at a small fireplace set in a corner of the house, opposite the direction of the prevailing wind. One of the most welcome and convenient items brought by traders to the region was the iron cooking grate, which allowed pots to be set above the coals, not just beside or among them. Eventually, the railroad brought still larger and heavier goods to the territory, and the grate was replaced by the wood-fired cookstove. Such blessings came last to the rude homesteads of Diamante, where they were not automatically accepted. Even after Jacobo's family acquired a cookstove and happily enjoyed the heat it gave, his mother Demetria persisted for years in cooking at the old corner fireplace.

A metes and bounds survey made in 1913 during the land-grant litigation described the Diamante tract as bounded on one side by *el banco del Apache*. Jacobo said he never heard any ridge called by that name but allowed one could have been. Certainly in the 1850s, and perhaps later, bands of Jicarilla Apache camped in the area, sometimes for whole seasons. They were trading partners with the Pueblo Indians at nearby Picuris and also with the villagers.

The villagers looked down on Indians, much as Anglos did. They were considered pagan, shiftless, dirty, and backward—all the usual under-class attributes. The Jicarilla, however, were at least credited with being useful. Like the Picuris, they made sturdy ceramic pots from clay deposits similar to the one at Diamante. They bartered their pots with the villagers, swapping a big *olla* for as much flour as it would hold, or a smaller, more ornamented piece for its volume in butter or lard. Until replaced by metal cookware brought in by Anglo traders, the Jicarilla pottery was widely used throughout the mountains.

People in villages more prosperous than Diamante, including Jacobo's future wife Eloisa, whose family lived opposite the church on the Las Trampas plaza, used to joke scornfully that the Romeros and their neighbors "must be *indios*." Their children, it was said, ran barefoot through the mountains like little savages. Even the adults took their meals squatting before the corner fireplace, dipping their tortillas in a common pot, without benefit of furniture or forks. "*Que bárbaro*," it was said, "*esa gente vive como indios*"—those folks live like Indians. The characterization struck a nerve. Even in old age Jacobo was vehement on the subject of Indian heritage. When a daughter asked if there were not a little Indian blood in the family, he struck the table with his fist and declared, "We are not *indio*, not a little bit!"

In fact his denial might have been more truthful, had it been less categorical. Many of the Hispanic people of the region can claim both

Indian and Spanish ancestry. Their forbears include not only Cortez and his countrymen but also the native people of what is now Mexico, who were first the victims, then the allies and subjects of the Spanish conquest. The genetic exchange continued in the northern province of New Mexico and later in the U.S. territory. It was common for a few individuals in any community—and in some cases the population of whole villages, like Anton Chico or Abiquiu—to have come as captives or fugitives from tribes on the periphery of the settlements.

It is sometimes hard for Anglos to understand that the state's native Hispanos defy easy categorization. To focus on their Indian heritage, or alternatively, to close discussion by saying that culturally they are Spanish and Mexican, misses an important point. Something happened in the soil of New Mexico. Isolated by broad deserts from their countrymen to the south, the *norteños* of New Mexico drew nourishment from the land in which they lived. People from other regions rarely appreciate that New Mexico was a frontier unlike any other in our national experience. While Virginia, Kentucky, or Missouri may have represented civilization's advancing edge for two or three generations, New Mexico remained a lonely and embattled frontier for three hundred years. It became *una patria*, a fatherland, in its own right.

To be sure, the people who wrung a living from Diamante's chilly meadows lived in many ways like the *indios* who gave the *banco del Apache* its name. Even more, they lived like generations of New Mexicans before them. They depended for all they had or hoped for on the strength in their arms, their capacity to work, and *la voluntad de Dios*. They knew their prayers might go unanswered, their work unrewarded. They were subject at every turn to the mountain storms that washed precious seed from the furrows or flattened crops, to the winter snow which at 9,000 feet accumulated several feet deep and lingered for months.

But the Romeros were not resigned to the limitations of their world. They began to look beyond the ridges that enfolded Diamante. With the encouragement of Presbyterian missionaries who plied the villages of the Sangre de Cristos, Narciso and Demetria, notwithstanding that they were both good Catholics, decided in about 1905 that Esequiel, their eldest son, should leave the mountains to become educated at Menaul, a Presbyterian school in Albuquerque, one of the territory's best.

The missionaries gave them a cardboard suitcase, a sheaf of enrollment papers, and money for the boy's train fare to the city. At sunrise on a clear September day Demetria, Esequiel, and several of the younger children, Jacobo included, set off by wagon for the rail station at Embudo, beside the Rio Grande. It took a full day to descend from the forests of Diamante through the woodlands and mesas to the scorched basalt canyon of the Big River. There they waited for the train. Toward sundown it arrived, took on water and wood, and they said their goodbyes and waved as Esequiel boarded the train, flimsy suitcase in his hand.

The locomotive hissed and pulled away. In a moment Esequiel reappeared at the window of the passenger car, waving as the belching locomotive filled the canyon with smoke. The train and its passengers were soon shrouded in a gray half-light, and Jacobo fixed in his mind that image of his older brother setting out on his adventure of opportunity—Esequiel, the family representative to a great and unknown world, waving bravely through the haze as the train disappeared.

The next day, early, Demetria, Jacobo, and the other children filled the wagon with a load of melons and turned the team toward home. Watermelons and musk melons grew well in the hot land near the river, but higher up in Las Trampas, El Valle, and Diamante, the summer nights were too cool to ripen them. Such sweet fresh fruit was a delicacy, and they had no trouble selling a portion of their load in each of the villages they passed. By the time they reached Diamante, they had made back all the money they had spent, and they still had melons for a feast.

They gathered for dinner as usual, placed the iron grate on the coals in the corner fireplace, and laid the clay griddle on top of it. Demetria made tortillas on the griddle. Emelia, the eldest girl, helped her set pots of beans and meat around the fire to boil. Living like *indios*, they lacked tables and chairs, and the family—thirteen now with the brother gone to Menaul—sat on blankets on the earthen floor, dipping their food from the pots with folds of tortilla. There was Narciso and Demetria. There was Amador, Avelino, Guillermo, Élfido, Juan de Jesús, Jacobo, and Demostenes. There was Emelia, Sofía, Magdalena, Franqui, and Julia, who was only a baby. After the meal, they sat together in a circle and brought out the melons.

They were starved for sweets, and the sugar in the fruit was as heady as wine. The more they ate, the louder they laughed, the higher and faster they chattered. Hardly anyone noticed when a tin of baking powder fell off the shelf beside the chimney.

Emelia put it back.

A few minutes later the baking powder fell again. "You didn't put it right," said Narciso.

"Yes I did."

"Put it again," he ordered. So Emelia put the can back and everybody watched to see that she placed it on the shelf securely. After only a moment they forgot about the baking powder. The melon was delicious and there was no limit to what they could eat. They spat the seeds into a glistening pile of rind in the center of the floor. The house was redolent with the syrupy smell. They joked and teased and wiped their hands on each other's clothes.

Then the can fell a third time.

No one spoke. They searched each other's faces in the lamplight and tasted the flat and bitter taste of dread, which leaked through the room like smoke blown down the chimney. Narciso broke the silence. "Something bad is going to happen to the family," he said solemnly.

Something did. Eight days later a letter came from Menaul that another student had punched Esequiel in the chest, and the blow had stopped his heart. He was dead. The family thought of *brujos*—witches, ghosts—and they marveled how the night of the melon feast had prepared them for the dismal news. The family made ready for another trip to Embudo. The body was to be shipped back by train, and with it they would haul a load of only sorrow on the long climb into the mountains.

5

Travels Without Maps

In the mountains the touch of death was never far away. An animal died or was killed somewhere in the valley nearly every day. You shot the cow, or, in the old-fashioned way, clubbed it with an ax or a maul, and you did it with dispatch. But never with grace. No cow or hog ever fell in the right position, and the aftermath of its death, the turning and bleeding and lugging around, was invariably messy and difficult. Killing a sheep was different. A sheep does not struggle or even protest its own death and accordingly does not merit a bullet. You straddle its back, grasp it by the lower jaw, pull back the head and slice the throat deeply with a knife, cutting to the spine if you can to be sure of severing the arteries. A chicken's death, meanwhile, was scarcely noticed; you simply swung it round by the head, casually, like a toy.

Some said there were signs when death came for humans. The baking powder falling from the shelf, for instance. Or almost any unexplained strange noise, like a cock crowing at midnight. But not everyone agreed about such things, least of all Jacobo and his wife, who held opposite views on all matters touching *brujería*. One evening as they finished dinner in their kitchen, their conversation turned to the subject of witchcraft.

Eloisa, known to us and all the neighbors as Liza, stated categorically that all talk of *brujos* was nonsense. Having raised twelve children on a mountain farmstead, she had seen a thing or two, and she allowed, not without a chuckle, that most *brujería* consisted simply of people playing jokes on each other. Jacobo offered no argument, and so she went on:

"I remember when I was a girl in Trampas there was an old lady who

lived alone, and people said she was *embrujada*—bewitched. One night this lady sees strange lights in the trees across the field from her house. The next night those lights are there again. And every night after that. She can see them out there across the field, where no lights are supposed to be. Sometimes the lights are still; other times they are moving. The old lady is very scared, but she can do nothing. She is old and too crippled to go across the field by herself to see what is the matter with those lights.

"But finally she cannot stand it anymore and she goes to her neighbor to ask help. He is an old man, almost as old as her, and he is half crippled too. But he says he will help her. So the next time she sees those lights, she calls to him and tells him to go across the field and see what they are. The old man goes. He is gone a long time. It is dark and he has to be very careful. And because he cannot walk very well, it takes him an hour to go across the field, another hour to come back. But he tells the old lady what he finds: *faroles* hanging in the trees. *No más*. Just lanterns. Probably young boys playing a trick. And that was all the *brujería* that there was."

Jacobo laughed. He seemed to implode, as though he did not want the laugh to escape. It was clear his sympathy in the story lay not with the old lady or the old man, but with the pranksters.

Liza fixed him with the same scolding stare she would give the boys who hung the lanterns. "And what about your brother?" she asked. "Remember when he thought he saw a *brujo* right out there in the road?" She pointed at the window, beyond which a security light bathed the road in yellow. "He ran inside to get the rifle, and ran back out and started shooting. But all he shot was the light of the moon on a puddle."

Jacobo shook his head, and his laugh continued to rumble. "Well, I can't say no," he smiled. "Many times what people say is a *brujo* is only a trick or something they imagine. Just the same, I cannot deny certain things that I have seen."

Solemnly he mentioned the death of Esequiel, which was announced the night of the melon feast, how the tin of baking powder fell three times from the shelf. "Was another time too," he said. "The rooster of a neighbor at Diamante crowed all one night, and my father said, 'Someone will die in that family within a year.' And that is what happened. One of the children get sick and die."

Liza gave him no credence. "You are crazy, old man. All the time we had chickens, our rooster would crow at night plenty, and nothing ever happened."

"Maybe that rooster was born from a machine," Jacobo rebutted. "Maybe all the roosters people get these days are born from machines, and they don't know what they are doing any more."

Liza laughed. "No, those chickens don't know too much," she said. "All they know is to eat and make eggs." She stood up and began to clear dishes from the table.

Jacobo was not ready to abandon the subject. "I cannot say," he began gravely, "that I have ever seen the lights of a witch, but my father was a serious man and he used to say that sometimes he saw them over the fields, and they would jump all of a sudden from one pasture to another.

Someone else who has seen them is Juan de Dios. He can tell you this story. He has told it to me many times, and each time the same. He does not change what he says, so I believe him."

Juan de Dios Romero was Jacobo's brother-in-law, the husband of Franqui, his youngest sister, but otherwise no close relation. For many years they had traveled together to and from "the sheeps" in Wyoming and other states. Jacobo had considerable respect for Juan de Dios. He marveled at his brother-in-law's curiosity about the world and especially his appetite for exploration and travel. Time meant nothing to Juan de Dios, Jacobo used to say. If he wanted to see something, he just went ahead to see it, no matter if it made him days late for being somewhere else.

Juan de Dios liked to travel alone, to go simply *paseando*, to see what he could see—for days or weeks, if weeks were needed. One spring, for instance, heading out to "the sheeps," he didn't buy a ticket for the train. He spent his money on a new saddle horse and rode from El Valle to a sheep ranch in the sagebrush plains south of Rawlins, Wyoming, where both he and Jacobo worked as herders. It was later that year, on the return—again, by horseback—from Rawlins to El Valle, that he had a close encounter with a witch.

Before he left Wyoming, he wrote a letter to his sister. She shared a house with him on the Llano de San Miguel, a string of broad fields and pastures on a slope overlooking the rest of El Valle. The letter said simply, "I am coming home. I do not know when I will get there." Three weeks or so after the letter arrived, a neighbor said to the sister, "Your brother will be home by noon."

"How do you know that?" she asked.

"That is what people down in the village are saying."

"How do they know?"

"I can't say, don't know."

The sister, and later Juan de Dios himself, inquired further to learn the source of the rumor, for indeed he arrived in El Valle about noon, after a very strange night on the trail. But they never did manage to track the rumor down. Its source seemed to lie in the *brujería* that beset Juan de Dios in the last leg of his trip.

The trip from Wyoming had passed slowly and pleasantly. In those days livery stables were still common, and Juan de Dios had no problem taking care of his horse whenever he passed the night in a town. Many nights, however, he slept out on the trail under the stars and hobbled his horse to graze nearby.

After many days of travel, Juan de Dios reached Taos. He continued south from the town, following the old Camino Militar, which descended the Taos plain through a rugged canyon toward the Rio Grande. About dusk he reached the village of Pilar, where the road met the Rio Grande. He found a meadow outside the village where his horse could graze, and he fixed himself a supper of canned meat and tortillas. He rested there for an hour or two.

Although it was a cloudy night with no stars or moon to guide him, he decided not to camp but to ride on. He was eager to be home.

He had not ridden far when he noticed a light that preceded him a considerable distance ahead. Sometimes it seemed to float, sometimes to bound. It turned off the main road and up the trail along the Rio Pueblo, where he intended to turn. He continued to follow it and was amazed how it turned with every bend in the trail.

When he came to a bridge over the river, the light seemed to pause, as though inviting him to approach. Juan de Dios thought of fleeing—and so did his horse. The animal cocked its ears, muscles tense, nostrils flared, breath heaving. Juan de Dios had only to touch heels to its ribs and the horse would have carried him far and fast from the annoying light.

But Juan de Dios was not a timid man. He had ridden from New Mexico to Wyoming and back. He did not shy from strange events, no matter how bizarre. Juan de Dios drew confidence, moreover, from an idea he'd given much thought to over the years. It was generally said in the villages that no one named Juan could be harmed by a witch. He would put that idea to the test. He rode forward.

His horse became more skittish the closer they came to the light. It refused to step onto the bridge. The bridge lacked side rails, and the horse was balking so badly that Juan de Dios feared the animal might lose its footing and fall off the bridge, taking him with it. And so he dismounted and coaxed the beast gently forward, leading it by the reins. The horse stamped and snorted, and the sound of its hooves boomed from the planks of the bridge. The light was no more than the length of a fence rail away when the horse reared, nearly breaking the reins. Juan de Dios was lucky to dodge a kick. The commotion seemed to disturb the light, and it floated farther ahead.

At times the light grew larger as they continued up the trail, turning now away from scattered ranchos of the Rio Pueblo to climb a narrow canyon. At other times it diminished.

Slowly the night passed, the light always a short distance ahead. The horse grew calmer, and Juan de Dios began to drowse as they plodded onward. About an hour before dawn, the horse became suddenly tense again and snapped Juan de Dios from his reverie. The light had stopped moving. It hovered two dozen yards away. He let the horse feel his spurs and rode up to it, reins taut. The light grew smaller as they approached, until it was no bigger than an apple. The horse was trembling. Juan de Dios reached out and cupped the light into his hand. It shone softly. He touched it with his other hand. Rubbed it gently. It had the feeling of dry, clean dirt. It crumbled and went out.

He rode on as the eastern sky above Trampas Peak grew light and reached El Valle about noon, where his sister, to his great surprise, had already prepared a sumptuous meal and his relatives had assembled to greet him. Everyone marveled at his strange adventure of the night before, and no one doubted that the light had been a witch.

"Years ago the people used to see too many *brujos*," said Liza. "They don't see so many now."

"Maybe too much has changed," Jacobo said. "Maybe that is why we don't have *brujos* like we used to." He gestured at the fluorescent tubes burning overhead. "We don't have these lights until the fifties or later, I think. And they don't bring the telephone or pave the highway through Trampas until in the sixties. Too much is different now. I don't think the *brujos* like it around here any more. Probably they move away."

"And where do you think they move to, old man?" Liza asked.

"Well . . . ," Jacobo stared a moment at the table before him. Then looked up, smiling. "Maybe Florida, California, Santa Fe. A lot of crazy things happening in those places. But maybe the *brujos* look around, and they don't find any place better to go. Could be they stay here and just retire. Like me."

"It is too bad for those *brujos* if they don't like it here anymore," rejoined Liza. "But for me it is much better. I would not go back to those days. The work was too hard."

Jacobo didn't argue. They'd covered that ground before. There wasn't much question whether modern conveniences like electricity and indoor plumbing had helped men or women more. The toil of childrearing on the homestead, washing clothes in great kettles outdoors beside the *ace-quia*, mending, feeding, and in autumn preserving buckets and baskets of food had been enough to cure any woman of nostalgia for the old days. But when the men began leaving each year for wage work outside the village, the women's burden increased. Then there was men's work as well as women's work to do.

But for the men—at least for those who welcomed time away from the family, who had an appetite for adventure—there was a positive side to the new regime. As they ventured into the world, they might, like Juan de Dios, go *paseando*.

The idea was not simply to travel, but to travel without agenda, open to the accidents of fate, much as an Australian goes *walkabout* or a German indulges *wanderlust*. For Jacobo, going *paseando* was a memorable pleasure of youth, when he was free to strike out into unknown territory, testing his luck—and pushing it—for days or weeks at a time, usually to learn he was equal to the obstacles he encountered, sometimes to find he was not.

In the years when we first knew Jacobo, Alex and I were going *paseando* too, and we used to measure ourselves against the stories the old man told us. Alex's travels took him for long periods to Alaska, where he was working on a new photographic project. I stayed closer to home, frequently backpacking or riding horseback in the Pecos high country, beyond the peaks that rose above the village..We were going *paseando* in a double sense. It was how we traveled *and* how we worked. As a photographer, Alex trusted in his luck. At times his plan was to have no plan, but to expose himself to whatever fortune would bring, and capture such photographs as were offered him.

My ramblings in the mountains had still less structure. I called them *research*, but wouldn't argue the point. I thought of them as hunting trips where I hoped to bag something to write about. I traveled alone, the better to take risks, to know my luck. When I started going on horseback, which somewhat increased the level of danger, Jacobo counseled me solicitously. It was plain I was a novice. "Keep your horse always tied," he said. "*Mejor contar las costillas que sus pasos sigiendolo*. Keep him tied and let him go hungry. It's better to count his ribs than your steps chasing after him." Even with the advice, I counted my steps a time or two, and came home once with ribs broken, an eye as black as a tar pit, and assorted other injuries from a horse wreck—or some other calamity. I'll never know because my loss of memory was permanent and total.

I had awakened at sundown in a high meadow, ignorant of my name, my past, and all geography. My horse, loaded with saddlebags and bedding, was tied by its picket rope to an aspen not far away. There was dried blood around my eye. I climbed in the saddle. My side hurt. My head was numb. I rode first one way, then another, hoping to get down from the ridge I was on and find water. In spite of discomfort and grogginess, I felt oddly exhilarated. The sunset was calm; the air was cool and dry; the night would be clear. So what if I was hurt. So what if I was didn't know who I was. I was alive!

The next morning at dawn I awoke with a start, as though a switch were thrown in my brain. Suddenly my memory returned to me. I knew my name and address. I knew Anne's name and address. I could divide, multiply, and name the capitals of most states. I could also remember the events of the previous day up to the point, in late morning, when I dismounted to drink from a stream five miles from where I woke up, mindless, at sunset. I never salvaged the least recollection of what happened in the eight hours after that. Nor was I able, in a day of tracking, to find the scene of the accident, or the hat, jacket, and glasses I had lost.

Two days later I was home again. Jacobo was amused, also concerned. He coached me more carefully about handling my horse, which, as horses go, had more than average cunning. "Too bad she is smarter than you," Jacobo said. "You got a problem there."

It was a problem I avoided in winter by backpacking, sometimes on snowshoes. The short days and serious cold were analogous to a rowdy horse—they reduced the margin for error. And the solitude meant that, if things went wrong, there was no one else who might give help, and no one else to blame. Being alone on those trips was instructive. I came to believe that moods were like letters—if you couldn't mail them, you didn't write them. Instead you shed the indulgent ups and downs of life in village or town and settled into a feeling of steadiness that lasted day after day, mile after mile. That small epiphany gave a hint, I thought, of the inner steadiness I sensed about Jacobo—he who had "followed the sheeps" for so many years, who now daily worked alone in his fields, in good weather and bad.

On one November trip, however, such steadiness as I'd attained proved shaky. Snow blanketed the mountains, but not so deeply that snowshoes were required. I hiked to within a mile or two of a junction of alpine divides and camped in a meadow beside an ice-hung stream. The next morning trudging up the trail in frozen boots, I saw, a hundred yards away through a screen of trees, a crumpled pyramid of metal at the foot of a broken spruce. I noticed odd bits of litter on the snow—a roll of tissue, a cushion, a cowboy hat.

The heap of metal was an airplane. There were four bodies in it, still in their seats, quite dead and quite frozen. My hands shook as I copied the number that was painted on the fuselage. The wind rose, and the noise of the empty forest grew oppressive, like a storm of static. My thoughts were drowned out. I talked to myself firmly and aloud, just to hear my own voice, just to keep control.

For the rest of the day I continued climbing, trying in vain to make a scheduled rendezvous with a party of game wardens, who would have a radio. But my strength was sapped by worry, and I stopped exhausted two miles and a mountain's width from where they were likely, but not certain, to have camped. That night I had a nightmare I had not dreamed since childhood.

In it, two abstract shapes fought and argued. One shape was large and male. It growled with the sound of an angry bass viol. The other shape snarled back in a female voice, that of a cello or viola bowed hard and discordantly. There was a third being in this dark *Fantasia*. It was small and skittered at the foot of the other two, squealing fearfully in the high register of a violin. The large shapes, blind to the small one and careening in their combat, were always on the verge of crushing it.

My nightmare was a rehearsal of guilt: I the child was responsible for my parents' arguing and would suffer the consequences. Only now, in the mountains, the dream logic stretched thinner. It drew from the plane crash an analog to childhood anxieties. At some deep level I felt responsible for the deaths in the forest. Cause and effect changed places. Since I found the corpses, they were *my fault*, at least until I told someone about them.

I packed up my camp in the first light of dawn. I hurried the dozen miles back to the trailhead on adrenalin strength, as though my pack had no weight. A forest ranger I knew was working on a truck outside his home in Peñasco, beside the highway. I reported everything to him. By early afternoon, I was back at home and lightheaded with relief.

The evacuation of the bodies and associated news coverage caused a stir in the village for several days. Jacobo quizzed me closely. I remember how long and firmly he looked me in the eye. He seemed to know already how my long night in the wilderness had gone.

"And after you find them, do you sleep that night?" he asked.

"Not very well, I had to camp between two drifts, and there was a big wind. It was cold, and I kept seeing them."

"I would not sleep either, not until I tell somebody about those *difuntos*."

"Yes," I said, "I didn't feel right until I got the word out. The next day I hiked to Santa Barbara and told La Floresta where to find them. Then I was okay."

"Yes, you got to tell the news. Those *difuntos* are fine until you know about them. Then you got to get them to their people."

My mountain trips were short, lasting usually less than a week, at most two. Alex, by contrast, was gone for months at a time, visiting Eskimo villages along the Bering Sea coast so isolated that advance arrangements were strictly a gamble. You arranged what you could; then you just went.

The trips seemed to diminish Alex's shyness. He grew bolder not just in what he did but in how he described it. He developed a fair skill at storytelling and seemed to enjoy the gatherings following each of his trips when Jacobo, Anne, and I questioned him about what he'd seen and done. After one such session I noted in my journal that Jacobo registered less surprise than I at one of Alex's strange encounters, no doubt, I thought, because his own meandering as a sheepherder had yielded many more.

Alex related how he hired a bush pilot to fly him from Bethel, the most substantial town in that part of far west Alaska, to Tununak, a tiny fishing and sealing village two hundred miles away. It turned out that the pilot was just up from the lower forty-eight and new to the Alaskan bush. Partly because of his inexperience, they flew into a dangerous storm. The pilot struggled to control the plane and fought to unfold an enormous air navigation map across the cramped cockpit. The noise of the engine deafened them both. He shouted to Alex, "I can take you back to Bethel. Or I can take you as close to Tununak as I can get, maybe here, to Tooksook Bay," and he pointed to a dot in a great blank expanse of map.

Alex chose the latter, thinking that it was safer to be on the ice than in a plane with a green pilot. He hoped he had written down somewhere a name he'd been given of a man who lived in Tooksook Bay, which lay across Nelson Island from Tununak.

With difficulty, the pilot found Tooksook, a cluster of shacks and kayak racks overlooking a frozen sea. Both night and the heart of the storm were approaching—a black wall of turbulence raging in from Siberia. The pilot set the plane down on a snow-packed strip of tundra, and Alex jumped out. The pilot unceremoniously pitched out Alex's gear after him, then without a word pulled shut the door. He gunned the engine, pivoted the plane, and roared into the sky. Alex stood alone with his duffel and camera case at the edge of the frozen runway. He watched his last connection with civilization drone into the darkness. There was no one in sight. Fog and foul weather advanced on a bitter wind. The stark, treeless Arctic wilderness spread around him.

"I felt kind of weird then," Alex said. "All I could do was walk toward the village."

"I know that feeling," said Jacobo, nodding gravely. He listened with approval as Alex related that the first house he came to belonged to a married Eskimo couple, ex-teachers from Anchorage who said they were getting back to their roots. They were glad to have company. Three days later an Eskimo friend from Tununak, whom Alex contacted by radio, drove by snowmobile across the frozen island, pulling a wooden sled. The sled was Alex's coach on the ride back to Tununak.

Things worked out. That was how it usually was when you travelled *paseando*, unconstrained by schedules or maps, with purpose loosely defined.

"Sometimes I been left in strange country like that," Jacobo offered. "I don't like it, but not much to do when it happens."

"Tell us what happened to you."

"Well, was a time in Utah they gave me a horse, two dogs, and two thousand sheep. I was no much but a kid. They tell me, take three days food and go down some canyons. I went down there looking for the place they say my partner will meet me, but I don't find it. I stayed lost for a week." He pondered the memory in silence a moment, his expression solemn. Then he brightened. "But better I remember the first time I leave El Valle. It was Juan de Dios and me. We go to herd for an uncle near Antonito. That was some good days, especially when I ride back on the train alone."

"How old were you?"

"Oh, a kid, *no más*. Maybe thirteen, fourteen, and Juan de Dios a little older. My father drive us to Antonito all the way in the buggy."

The buggy, he said, was the first vehicle the family owned that had springs. The springs smoothed the ride over the tooth-rattling washboards that marred the dirt roads. Also its wheels were narrow, not like the clumsy farm wagons. You could miss the rocks and go fast, riding in genuine comfort. Jacobo's father bought the buggy with money he earned as a section hand for the Atchison Topeka and Santa Fe Railroad. He may have been among the first to leave the village for cash wages.

Narciso Romero set out from El Valle some time in the first decade of the century, leading a burro packed with supplies. He trekked for four or five days, first across the mountains to Mora, then up and over Raton Pass, and onto the plains of southeastern Colorado. He reported to an AT&SF section camp in the lonely, flat country near Timpas Creek and told the foreman he wanted work. The next morning he was swinging a maul and spiking ties. The hard labor didn't pay much, but any cash seemed a lot in those days, and the wages accumulated. They led eventually to the purchase not just of a buggy but of a farm lower down in El Valle on good, productive land. The family moved out of Diamante and was well settled on the new land when Jacobo, barely a teenager, set out for the sheep ranges above Antonito in the company of his father and Juan de Dios.

"We cross the Rio Grande at Rinconada, which was the only bridge for many miles north and south, then pass the night on the edge of the plains, above the canyon. Next day, we go as far as Tres Piedras, and the day after, Antonito."

Jacobo's uncle was a *partidario*. He sharecropped sheep. Although he may have owned a portion of his herd, most of his animals belonged to someone else, a merchant or large property owner. At the end of the grazing season, he owed rent for the use of those animals which he paid in the form of so much wool and so many lambs. Depending on how many of the herd he had lost to disease, storms, and predators, he might take home a profit from his year to nine months on the range, or more often, he found himself in debt to the company store, where by contract he was obliged to supply himself.

The finer points of the *partido* system, however, were lost on Jacobo, who soon found himself, as the youngest member of the outfit, fully occupied with the drudgery of camp life. He collected wood and built fires, cooked pots of beans, broke and moved camp. Periodically he stood guard over the skittish sheep, several thousand in number, which made a sound when they ate like a chorus of dull crickets. Jacobo never knew that year whether his uncle made money or lost it, partly because his uncle, a bachelor, never spoke except to exchange vital information.

"He don't talk for nothing. If I ask a question, he act like he don't hear me. So we never talk to pass the time, and Juan de Dios and me don't talk when he is there. We just sit, keeping quiet, and we never know if he is happy with the work we are doing or if he don't like us at all. That was not very good. I used to cry for my mama when I got there. I was not happy to be with that uncle."

The first and nearly only time the uncle made his feelings known occurred soon after Jacobo and Juan de Dios arrived in camp. They were awakened in the middle of the night by the winds of a late spring blizzard. The uncle left the tent to check on the sheep. Soon he was back ordering the boys to pull on their clothes and saddle horses. The sheep had run off. They had to find them quickly and hold them, before the storm scattered them to the ends of the earth.

Each left camp in a different direction angling down wind, as they guessed the sheep had done. They rode in pitch darkness and bitter cold. Jacobo crossed two ridges and thought he heard the sheep. Moments later the clouds broke and he caught a glimpse in the faint moonlight of a large band of sheep scattered across a meadow. It may not have been the whole herd but was at least more than half. To his relief, the sheep had settled down and were still. Jacobo, astride his horse and back to the wind, resolved to stand guard over them the night long, no matter how cold or weary he became. His uncle, like it or not, would have to acknowledge him.

The night wore on, and Jacobo suffered the worst cold and weariness he'd ever known. An hour before dawn, he heard a rider approach through the darkness. It was his uncle, whose eyes glared with anger as he rode past him, continuing down into the sheep, which oddly did not stir as he rode among them. The uncle called Jacobo's name. Jacobo followed him into the meadow. "Is this what you were watching all night?" he demanded.

To his horror Jacobo saw that the sheep, so white and still, were, in fact, not sheep. What he had guarded the night long was bushes of snow-covered sagebrush. Between the bushes, leading away from camp, he saw the hours-old, snow-filled tracks of the herd.

They spent the next two days gathering the band back together as best they could. They found most of the animals, but not all of them, and Jacobo recovered some, but not all, of his damaged pride.

At the end of the summer his uncle paid him his wages: three silver dollars, the most money he had ever touched that belonged to him. Juan de Dios had left for El Valle a week or two earlier, and so his uncle put him on the train at Antonito alone. It was a relief to leave his uncle and a moment of triumph to set out on his first solitary journey.

"I remember there were many people at the depot, selling tamales, *carne seca*, any kind of food. Everybody was pushing and calling. And the train made a lot of noise too.

"I get on the train and lean out the window. There is a man right there on the siding, and he say, 'You better buy some tamales so you don't go hungry.' Then the train start to pull out. So I say, '*Bueno, dame dos tamales.*' And the train is moving now so he has to run a little to keep up. But he hands me the tamales and I take them. And he say, 'Five cents.'

"And now the train is almost to the end of the depot, and I don't give him nothing. The man curse me. He shake his fist and shout. But I just smile, and I take a bite of that tamale." Closing his eyes, Jacobo licked his lips. "That was a good tamale," he said. "I don't think I ever have another any better. But I was a bad boy. I was a little crooked in those days."

Soon it was Jacobo's turn to be surprised. When the train pulled into Barranca Station, in Taos County, the conductor told him to get off. He

did as he was told. Barranca was a wooden two-room oasis at the edge of an immense sagebrush plain. At that time, several years before construction of Taos Junction, Barranca was the closest rail stop to the town of Taos, which lay twenty-five miles away by stage on the far side of the Rio Grande gorge. Jacobo was the only passenger to leave the train. Two canvas sacks and a wooden crate were also thrown off, and the brakeman hurried from car to car setting the retainers for the long descent to Embudo.

The brakeman shouted to the conductor, who called to the engineer. There was a blast of air as the brakes released. Jacobo watched with despair as the train began to pull away. He looked for the conductor, to appeal to him. But the conductor was already at the far end of the train, looking away. The train gained speed and rumbled off, rails clacking, headed for Embudo and the far-off, sheltered canyon of the Rio Grande. Embudo was his station, close to home, in land that he knew.

A solitary stationhand dragged the canvas sacks and the wooden crate into the freight room, then returned to the office and shut the door. He said nothing to the baggageless, bristle-haired boy who stank of sheep.

Jacobo looked around. He stood on the edge of a sagebrush plain in the middle of God knew where. The plain was twice striped: once thinly and darkly by the tracks of the railroad and once by a band of black basalt, which was all he could see of the rimrock of the gorge of the Rio Grande. Mountains bounded the plain in every direction, those in the southeast being the most jagged against the sky. They were the mountains that held his home, or at least he thought so, and looking at them he remembered what his uncle had said as he pressed the train ticket and the three silver dollars into his hand: "After the station you will see the sierra," he said, "and know which way to walk."

In the excitement of the moment he had paid little attention to his uncle, whose grumbling he had learned to ignore. But now Jacobo realized he should have taken warning from what his uncle said. His uncle had bought him a ticket only as far as Barranca, a full stop before Embudo. Maybe his uncle hadn't known better. Maybe he was just cheap. Or maybe he had reasoned that since Embudo was deep in the canyon, where the high peaks were hidden from view, Jacobo might walk the wrong way and get lost. Whatever the reason, Jacobo, barely a teenager, now faced a long trek in unfamiliar territory.

He realized that he could stay at the station, sleep under the eaves, and buy passage on the next train, tomorrow. But that would leave time to kill, and he might as well kill it walking. Besides, the three dollars in his pocket had been there only since morning. They were scarcely warm. They were the only dollars he had ever earned and he was not yet ready to spend the first cent of them, least of all on a train. He had already ridden the train.

A road departed the station southward, paralleling the tracks. He reasoned that the tracks had to lead to Embudo, and from there he knew his way. He guessed it would take close to two days to walk home, unless he hitched a ride on a wagon. His coat was warm and, besides the three silver dollars in his pocket, he had a clasp knife and a can of sardines. A sheepherder now, not a child, he set out toward the rocky cedar and piñon brakes that gave way to the canyon. He was not in a hurry. He had too far to go to be in a hurry.

Walking Canto

Up the known slope, which lengthens each year.

Distances get longer with age.

These days it is a journey to climb from where quelites *grow by the river, through the fields, to the house.*

The heat of the sun heavies your step, the same as when you wandered in the desert.

Think about 1914. You remember. You took the narrow gauge to Santa Fe, then the big train through Albuquerque to Williams. A day's ride by stage and bus brought you to Panguitch, Utah, where the gringo boss met you in an open Ford. Neither of you said much in the language of the other as you drove to the ranch near Antimony, on the edge of the Aquarius Plateau.

Next morning the boss gives you two thousand sheep, three days food, and points east. "Follow that canyon for two and a half, three days, then go up the big canyon on your right, as far as the ruined house. There'll be an orchard. Wait there. Your partner will come with wagon and supplies."

You are seventeen.

You and the woolly herd descend into the canyon. The sun is a weight, pushing you down. A ranch hand has whispered, "These canyons go to a big river they call the Colorado. But nobody here has been that far."

You go down. The walls close in. A stripe of sky rides between the rims. You are no longer on the earth but in it, like dirt in the cracks of your skin.

Toward noon on the second day you begin to watch for the big side canyon. There is none.

By nightfall of the third day you know you are lost. You have passed the big canyon, or it never existed. The redrock surrounds you. The sheep are footsore and restless, the dogs hungry. You eat the last of the jerky.

Next morning you debate where to go. You cannot stay where you are; there is no grass. You go forward, toward the Colorado.

By midday, the taste of fear is constant in your throat. Suddenly you heart beats fast. Up ahead, you see herders!

You try not to show how scared you've been. The herders tell you, "Muchacho, you're lost." You say, "Claro que sí, but where's the canyon with the orchard?" They argue among themselves. No one seems to know. Finally the one with rotten teeth says, "You passed it on your first or second day."

So you turn the herd.

You push them at a trot and find the canyon mouth by moonlight. Next day you drive them to the dead orchard and its empty shack. There is a spring, but no partner or supplies.

You have one more piece of bread, which you eat at sunrise, watching the trail. The herd straggles into thickets and narrow draws. You make no effort to retrieve them. Slowly the shadows shorten, disappear, then grow out again from the other canyon wall.

At sundown, a wagon comes creaking down the trail.

Turns out your partner is a gringo. In English he says, "I was lost three days on the rimrock. Couldn't find where to come down."

And you say, in Spanish, "Somos los dos pendejos. We don't know this country, and we got no business being here." The gringo doesn't understand. So you say, in English, "Fools!" You know that word. "You and me are both fools." Then you make a fire for the bacon.

You stay five months that winter. Every ten days the boss leaves beans, canned peaches, and bread at a crumbling shack a day's ride away. But you never see him. And the bread always spoils.

That's how it was in Utah. And later in Wyoming. Beans in the camp pot. Sheep, dogs, and weather.

And now, so much later, you shamble behind the wife, knees aching, the sun like the sun of the desert on your shoulder, no stink of sheep about you now, no creak from saddle or harness, no panting from eager dogs. You have your old man's mules—a pair of canes, you have a bucket of lambsquarters for the evening meal, and you have ranks of witless lambs still bleating in your mind.

6

Intactness

Jacobo was the first friend any of us had who was not a capitalist, but it took us a long time to understand that.

From 1975 onward, researching my book, I used to go to villages talking to people—conducting interviews, you might say, although what I did was casual and impressionistic by academic standards. The people who talked with me generally welcomed my interest but were also reticent. When my questions touched on the particular character of the land and its people, they would urge me, gently, to "talk to my grandmother," or "my uncle," or "the old man down the road. He is old but still remembers." Often there was a hint of reverence in the way the old people were mentioned, and I remember thinking it was like the way people in my family used to talk about dead heroes from the Civil War. I wasn't used to so much deference toward the living. Where I came from, old people were honored, often indulged, but only the working generation was a source of authority.

Then New Mexico. I began to wonder if the analogy between old Hispanos and dead southerners wasn't more accurate than I suspected. Maybe the changes in the village world between old ways and new paralleled those in the Old South, where a society was torn to pieces and scarcely put together again.

An old-timer in Mora described the magnitude of the change in a few sentences: "We used to take the cattle to the mountains as soon as the fields were ready to plow. Sometimes we'd have to dig steps in the snow to get them over the divide, and while we stay up there, we don't have sleeping bags and fancy things. We just make two big fires and lay the horse blanket and saddle down between them, and sleep there in our slickers.

Then, after we harvest the hay and wheat and other crops, we bring the cattle down again, and the fields were open to all the animals, and they stayed that way all winter. You could have no land—just a house—and still raise your cows and horses. Even the poorest family had twenty head. There were no fences, see? People were not selfish the way they are now. Today every monkey has his swing, and he just stays on that."

No barbed wire. Open fields. No Forest Service in the mountains with limits and regulations. Every man a farmer and rancher like every other. Every woman, like every other, making do with what her family's fields and animals yielded. What you did not own you might freely borrow. Neighbors charged no rent. There was no *envidia*, say the oldtimers. No envy. And almost no cash. If there was not always sufficiency, there at least was equality.

That was the old way, which the people I talked to, young and old, seemed to agree was the *true* way. Not that they wanted to return to it, or greatly idealize it. They were realistic about the hardship, isolation, and poverty of the villages in the old days, but they spoke of those things as though saying, "This is who we are and where we come from, and only the old folks who remember how it was before cash drove out barter, before Minnesota flour drove out local wheat, before the land grants were lost to Anglos—only the old ones really know what these villages mean."

The old ones, they were saying, had known a world that no longer existed. I imagined that world as a place physically different from what could be seen now. I thought of it as a remote valley that had defined a watershed of its own. A river flowed out from it toward Mexico, but the current was modest and sank underground in stretches of desert. Then, a century and a half ago, tectonic events occurred: the War of 1846, arrival of the railroads, connection to distant markets, availability of manufactured goods. A drama unfolded that had been repeated countless times before—and since. The valley watershed was "captured" by a larger river—the cash-based industrial economy of not just the United States but the western world. And from this new river everyone in the mountains has since drunk.

Among the living, only Jacobo's generation had tasted the older stream. They had been born and raised outside the economic Amazon, in a land where time was not confused with money and where money, by itself, was not considered unequivocally good. Their generation was the

last to tend its ideas, like its sheep, in valleys remote from the markets of the world. Jacobo, I eventually learned, may not have been exceptional because he spoke feelingly of the bygone days—there were many who did that. But he may have been exceptional because his good health and vigor enabled him to live out their values for so long.

Consider the making of *manojos*, sheaves of grass.

One afternoon in haying season Alex calls at the Romero house. Only Liza is there.

"Where is Jacobo?"

"He went to the river, but he should be back by now. I don't know what is the matter."

Liza kept a pair of binoculars on top of the refrigerator. She takes them to the porch and together she and Alex scan the fields. From the porch in winter you could see nearly all of the roughly thirty irrigated acres the old man managed, most of which he owned, and some, like the Americanos', he simply used. But in summer with the cottonwoods in leaf, large areas are hidden from view.

They see no sign of Jacobo.

"I'll see if I can find him," Alex says and starts down the path to the river.

He passes Jacobo's "office" and crosses the arroyo that serves as the household dump, then sets out across the farm's largest field, where the hay is waist high and ripe for cutting. At the foot of the field the path descends a low bluff to the river. The old man has fashioned a plank footbridge from scavenged boards and beams. Crooked handrails of peeled aspen run waist-high along both sides of the bridge, testimony to Jacobo's lack of confidence in his arthritic knees and to the energy with which he shapes the land to meet his needs. There are other bridges in the village, but none with handrails.

Jacobo is not at the crossing nor at the log gristmill on the other side. He built the mill many decades earlier and for years ground the valley's grains there. But the millstones have not turned since his children were young, and the mill now stores only memories and hay. Alex continues through the river pasture, which is cropped low by the cows, and edges uphill to avoid the irrigation waters the old man has set loose. Finally, near the fencegate, where he tops a swell of meadow, he sees the old man's body.

It lies stomach down, beside a fallen shovel. It does not move. The sight is like a fist in the chest. The old man must be dead. The heart in mid task has stopped. Alex approaches, reminding himself that of the people he knows, Jacobo most of all should die in harness. Softly now, "Jacobo?"

No answer.

Alex stands over him. "Jacobo?"

"Jacobo?"

The grizzled head moves. A muffled voice: "What?"

Heavily, like a walrus climbing a rock, Jacobo lifts himself to hands and knees. Looks at Alex, blinking.

"You were sleeping?"

"Resting a little." With the help of his canes he stands.

"I thought you were dead."

"Me?" Jacobo blinks some more. "Yah, maybe so. But only like a cat, just trying it out. Seems to me it was okay." He looks toward the sun. "It is late. Let's go to the house."

They return through the pasture, past the mill, across the bridge, up the long slope to the house. A giant cottonwood, not the narrow-leaved variety that grows in colonies along the river, but a towering, round-crowned Rio Grande cottonwood with heart-shaped leaves endlessly rustling, looms before the house. Lightning or some other trauma af-flicted the tree in its youth, for its trunk is split into a cavity big enough to

stand in. The woody cave serves the old man as a tool closet, and he hangs his shovel there between the hay rake and a coil of wire.

They step across the *acequia*, which bathes the foot of the tree. It runs in an arc before the two houses, Jacobo's and Liza's on the left, Lalo's on the right, which is really not a house anymore but a warehouse of tools and tack and old machinery. They settle on the porch, Jacobo in his favorite chair, a truck seat on wooden blocks which is low enough for him to remove his boots with ease. Liza also takes a chair as kittens scuffle between the legs of the wringer washer and hummingbirds scold among the flowers by the fence.

Except at night or in the grip of winter, you live outdoors in the village, beside the houses, not in them, and this deep porch, sheltered by the angle of the houses and shaded by the great tree, is a kind of room without walls, welcoming and quiet.

Years ago, however, when the Romero family was growing, peacefulness was a rare thing. The yard between the houses rang with the shouts and endless squabbling of children. Jacobo and Liza had twelve, plus two who died in infancy, and Jacobo's brother Juan de Jesús and wife and children lived in what is now Lalo's house, alongside the ditch, and brother Guillermo raised his brood in another house, now gone, that stood behind the others, across the road on the cut bank where Jacobo mounts his horse. Every meal was bedlam. Food was a commodity like firewood. It entered the house in great quantity, and therein vanished amid heat and a chorus of noises. With so many children, the domestic duties of cooking, washing, mending, canning, cleaning, nursing, and general mothering never ceased.

And because Jacobo was absent in Wyoming through the busiest part of the year, Liza bore not only domestic duties but the farm tasks as well. None of the men in the valley was any tougher or harder working than she. She could plow, plant, harvest, and slaughter. It was thanks to her iron constitution and relentless attention that she and her family not only survived the grueling years but, in the inconspicuous way of the villages, even prospered.

She never lost the habit of vigilance. When Jacobo talks about the business of the farm, she considers every word.

Alex asks, "When will you cut the hay, Jacobo?"

"Tomás says he will be ready about noon tomorrow."

"And you, old man, will you be ready?" asks Liza.

"Maybe. Not too much to do."

"Tomás don't want to wait when he brings the tractor."

"Maybe I can help," Alex offers, thinking both of help and photographs.

"Sure. We can get everything ready."

"What time will you start?"

"Oh, sunup."

Dawn came cool but without frost, and Alex found Jacobo on the porch sharpening a hand sickle with a flat metal file. The tightly curved blade, black with age and use, gleamed where the file had touched it.

"Morning. *¿Que está haciendo?*"

"Getting ready *la hoz*." He tested the blade of the sickle with a slow, broad thumb. Alex took a seat, and the old man continued, "Used to be, we had no tractors, nor mowers for the horses to pull, so we cut the wheat and oats and barley with these. Many people working, neighbors, men and women, children too. First we do one family's field, then another." The old man stroked the blade a few times more with the file. "We had another tool that you use for cutting grain, but I don't remember the name in English."

"Maybe *scythe?*"

"That's it. I never can say that word. The people in this place had a few of those, but not too many. Mostly we use the *hozito*, which everybody can use even if they are not too strong." He pulled a wool watchman's cap over his head and rose to leave. "Now maybe we can make some *manojos*."

He led Alex along the road and through a gate to a small orchard of aging trees heavy with apples. At the bottom of the orchard a second gate opened into a larger field where waist-high grasses rustled. This was the first field Tomás would cut, provided there was still no sign of rain by afternoon.

It was generally accepted that tractors wasted a certain amount of the crop. The cutter was an expensive piece of machinery and easily damaged, so the operator gave ample berth to fences, trees, ditches and other hazards both seen and suspected, with the result that the finished field had the look of a bad haircut: swatches of grass stuck out in this place and that, and the whole field was shaggy around the edges. Also wasted was the hay pressed irretrievably to the ground under the wheels of the tractor on its first circuit of the field, with the result that the average cutting operation might leave in the field the equivalent of several bales of unharvested hay. Even with large additional inputs of labor and machinery—to rake the hay, bale, and haul it away—those bales would still fetch no more than a couple of dollars each, and so the small amount of waste was of no particular concern. In fact, if cattle were turned into the field after haying, they would eat most of what the tractor had missed and there would be little net waste at all.

So went the thinking of most farmers in the village, including us. There was little variation. By adding fertilizer to the calculus of costs and benefits, one might develop a different routine, but almost no one did. It took cash to buy fertilizer and cash was immediate and tangible; the future return on its expenditure was as insubstantial as the talk of salesmen.

But there was another way to depart from the accepted norm. It was Jacobo's way, the way of the old days. Calculations of production efficiency make sense only if their results can be expressed in a single set of terms—dollars and cents. Jacobo grew up learning a simpler, more fundamental arithmetic—the arithmetic of completeness. Is all the land plowed that can be plowed? Sown? Harvested? Are the grain bins full? The hay barn? The root cellar? Are the livestock fat? One looks out over a field or a farm and takes its measure. Where the work is complete, it is seen to be so: the parts fit together in an intact whole. There is no acceptable alternative.

In the old days the family might consider itself secure only if the wholeness of the home and farm were intact. With the exception of a few fruits and vegetables, notably chile, which were obtained through barter with villagers from lower elevations, the farm had to be self-sufficient. What the family didn't make or grow, it didn't have.

And so a man like Jacobo, who grew up in the old days, under the old terms of existence, carried around in him a sense of necessity that preceded other levels of judgment. Alex and I struggled a long time to find a phrase to express this. Finally Alex said the old man had "an eye for intactness." Perhaps we can't get closer than that. If Jacobo looked across his fields and saw raggedness and incompleteness, the sight was jarring, even offensive. It was proof that the parts of his farm did not mesh, that the whole was not intact. The prospect that hay might lie wasted after harvest was an aesthetic as much as an economic affront, which required correction, even if the result of his efforts—in equivalent cash, net, after labor—were negative. The old man, to the limit of his strength, was driven to make things *look right*. And he expected his neighbors to judge him, as he judged himself, by the look of his land.

In the case of the *manojos* he wanted to make things look right even before it was evident they looked wrong. He aimed to harvest the hay by the pasture gate, as well as the tall grasses that grew in the old wagon ruts that led into the field. It was hay that the tractor would press down or fail to cut.

A *manojo* is a bundle, a sheaf. Stooped over, the old man began cutting handfuls of the tall grasses with short, jerking movements of the sickle.

The keenly whetted blade ripped through the stalks, and soon it dripped with dew.

The old man lay the cut stalks in a pile. When the pile was nearly as big around as the grass was tall, he selected several of the longest, stoutest stalks and passed them crosswise beneath the bundle. Then he drew the ends of the long stalks together and cinched the pile at the waist. He tied the stalks that bound the sheaf in a simple knot, and for an instant, his thick, twisted fingers, now coated with seed and chaff, worked nimbly. Without pausing, he took up the *hoz* again, and *rip, rip,* continued cutting toward the gate.

Alex marveled at the old man's dexterity and the ancient beauty of the finished sheaves. Once or twice he tried to tie a sheaf, but the stalks broke in the knot or the knot slipped. Jacobo gave no instruction. Like other old-timers in the valley he taught by example, not by words. Learning was elective. If Alex wished to make *manojos* correctly, he would study Jacobo more carefully. If not, he might do as he pleased. Alex watched as the small pile of bundles grew. Each *manojo* was light yet substantial, simple yet exceptional. Alex stood back and raised the camera. As he focused, he wondered if these might be the last *manojos* made in El Valle.

By midmorning it was a certainty Tomás would cut. The sun and breeze had carried off the dew. No clouds hung above the peaks, nor anywhere else in the sky. The entrance to the field and the borders of the wagon track were neatly trimmed. A cluster of *manojos* leaned against the fence, and others lay stacked beside the hedgerow.

Later, after Jacobo sat down to his midday meal, Alex returned to the field and photographed the sheaves against the fence. You feel, in the picture, the warmth of the September sun on your neck, the stillness and breadth of the valley, and looking into the distance, you can appreciate the smallness of the old man's painstaking, hand-powered labor in the sweep of the mountain environment. The picture was taken in 1978, but the *manojos* against the fence and the uncluttered, pastoral look of the landscape might belong to an earlier century.

But there are clues that place the image exactly in its own time. Not least is the metal wire that holds the latch of the fence gate. And the iron nails that invisibly bind the rails to their posts. But most persuasive is the texture of the vegetation in the distance: the swell of willows by the river,

the clustered oaks at the foot of the forest, the density of the forest itself.

I've looked for old photographs of El Valle and found none. But views of Las Trampas, Santa Fe, Santa Cruz, and other towns at the turn of the century show landscapes with no suggestion of bounty, landscapes that have been scoured and beaten. The lushness in Alex's photograph places it decades after World War II, which is to say, after the village herds of sheep and goats had been exchanged for relatively fewer cattle, after self-sufficiency had yielded to the dollar, after the population of the village had declined as though from an epidemic. It was an epidemic of economic change.

Seventy-five or a hundred years ago, when the old ways were still intact and the making of *manojos* was a current skill, the village supported quadruple or quintuple the number of people who live there now, and the fat of the land had long since been consumed. Particularly in the hard years of drought, people gnawed the gristle and the bone.

When Jacobo was growing up there was no riot of vegetation along the acequias, no thick underbrush in the arroyo thickets. The willows, alders, wild plums, and even junipers were pruned to the height a goat could reach. Wild roses and grass stubble succumbed to the free-ranging hogs. Draft horses and milk cows, grazing the hills close by the houses, examined every growing thing, and what they did not eat the sheep consumed, as herders turned them out from the barns in the morning and returned them every day as the sun went down.

The herders were usually young boys, boys like Jacobo when he was ten, often barefoot, accustomed to trailing behind the livestock and letting the herd dogs do the work, accustomed, in Jacobo's case, to passing the hours while the animals grazed by winging stones at trees and other targets from a leather sling. The sling was his principal toy and prized possession. Patrolling the forest a mile or two from the village, he was the scourge of rabbits, squirrels, and porcupines.

"I sure could hit 'em," the old man used to brag, and he'd squint and cock his throwing arm to show he still knew how to do it. "David killed Goliath with one of these," he smiled, "and when I was a boy, I stayed ready in case I would have to, too."

Day after day the prospective giant killer wandered the mountains with his charge of sheep and goats. Often he'd meet other children similarly at work, and they would spin tops or match skills with their slings while the

herds mingled and strayed. But the mountain quiet was deceiving. The forest in which they passed their half-indolent days was changing. Not only was its productivity declining from overuse, but outsiders were taking hold of it. By the time Jacobo was ten, the hills and mesas surrounding Trampas, El Valle, and Diamante had ceased to be the common possession of the heirs of the Las Trampas Land Grant. Unbeknownst to the villagers, a group of Anglo land speculators had purchased title to the grant, and their one dream was to sell it at a profit. As Jacobo and his friends stalked imaginary Goliaths, unseen real ones were sacking the village.

As an old man, Jacobo refused to dwell on the afflictions of the past. What was done was done; now was now. He lived adaptively, in the present. It was his nature to reconcile the past with the present as efficiently as he could and then move to more current matters. He explained *brujos* that way: he knew from personal experience that witches used to exist; but they didn't anymore; therefore, they must have died, retired, or gone elsewhere. So too with the old ways surrendering to the new: life is change. Nothing stays the same. No need to go into details. He could point to others who became obsessed with details and never recovered.

But the details interested me. In the years I knew Jacobo I delved into the history of the Las Trampas Land Grant and the transformation of the villages as deeply as I could. In his presence, though, I was careful not to show my obsession too plainly.

Perhaps it is enough to know that the "selling" of the Las Trampas Land Grant was a sordid chapter in the history of New Mexico. It is almost impossible not to feel outrage at what happened. Rather than protecting the rights of unsophisticated citizens, the law and the U.S. courts became active agents for their dispossession and further impoverishment. And the same wretched drama was repeated over and over throughout the Hispanic homeland.

As dire as the land grant story was, however, it was by no means the only force behind the changes in the village world. At the broadest scale, New Mexico was then still forging its connections to the great markets of the industrial world—and the industrial world was still developing New Mexico as a market for its products. Subsistence agriculture could not resist the advance of cash and capitalism any more than farmers could resist the change of seasons. Cash was a vegetal force. It penetrated the mountains the way tree roots probe a granite fissure.

The more I studied, the more I respected Jacobo's disinclination to explain why things changed. There were too many causes, and none existed independent of the others. There was the loss of the land grants; there was the way cash changed people's ideas about value, as well as their perceptions of their needs. There was the rise of commercial logging and grazing, as well as other industries that made cash wages available. There was also the booming population of the villages, whose demands on the land accelerated its decline, which, in turn, fed other changes, including the expanding power of the Forest Service. The chain of cause and effect went on and on, sometimes turning back on itself and tightening, binding the villages in its knot. Tens of thousands of people left the mountains for wage work, their only alternative. Most left forever.

Life is change. The old man waves his hand and dismisses history as being not impossible to dissect, but unrewarding. The present, by contrast, needs immediate attention. Is the calf born? Are the neighbors home? Do you want to hear a story?

There is a subtext to this tale of change and transformation. It centers on the people whose lives encompassed the changes, people as different from the people of the present as the old days were different from the conditions we live in now.

It took me a long time to realize Jacobo was not a capitalist because I had to learn first that I, unconsciously, was one. I had to understand how I'd been shaped by the wallet in my pocket, by the checks I wrote at the grocery store and the bills I paid each month. It is no easy thing for me to imagine what life would be like in a world without banks or credit. To imagine relying entirely on markets where little paper money changes hands, where barter is the main means of commerce. To imagine a frame of mind in which the answer to the question "What's it worth?" is not expressed in dollars and cents, where the question itself is rarely asked.

This is not to say that a man like Jacobo, whose values formed before cash became king, was naive about money. In fact, he understood it well. He worked year after year as a herder in Wyoming for the sake of it. But it is one thing to understand cash, and quite another to surrender to its imperatives. Jacobo's goals were material, but not material alone. They were shaped, in large measure, by love of land.

The death of his parents forced him to act. His father Narciso died first, and some years later Demetria passed away, with the result that ownership of the family property passed in more or less equal shares to the surviving children. The sons got the land. The daughters got the house.

There were five sons left. Esequiel died at Menaul; Demostenes succumbed to illness in his teenage years; Avelino went overseas as a doughboy in World War I and never came home. (It is not thought he was felled by battle or disease; more likely he died in a fight with another soldier.) Those remaining—Jacobo, Amador, Élfido, Guillermo, and Juan de

Jesús—received equal portions of the fields, but their portions did not follow fence lines or any other manageable boundary. The new situation made practical use of the land extremely difficult.

Still more difficult were the arrangements for the house. Each daughter became the owner of a single room: this one belonged to Sophía, that one to Franqui, the next to Julia, and so on. It was an impossible situation. Jacobo resolved to buy his siblings out.

For that reason, as well as for the year-to-year survival of his family, he worked hard for cash and saved it. Through the thirties and into the forties he purchased the main house from his sisters, room by room, and all of the fields save those that Amador, living next door, inherited or purchased just upstream of him. Last of all, in the late 1940s, Juan de Jesús resolved to sell the house he'd come to own, adjacent to Jacobo's, facing the ditch. But Jacobo, at the time, had no money to buy it. He was paying tuitions to Presbyterian boarding schools in Santa Fe and Albuquerque, as his parents had briefly done, so that his children might be educated. Fortunately, Lalo, Jacobo's oldest son, who was newly home from service as a G.I. in the Pacific, came to the rescue. Lalo traded Juan de Jesús a car and three hundred dollars for the house. Now the homeplace, the object of all Jacobo's striving for intactness, was complete.

When I walked in the hills around the village, I used to follow the same trails where Jacobo herded sheep and goats as a boy. At sundown, returning home, I'd try to imagine the boy gazing at the village from the crest of the final ridge. The sheep and goats straggle forward, eager to drink at the *acequia* and to feel the safety of the barn. The dogs lie in the dust panting, their day's job done. The landscape the boy sees is relatively less green than it is today. Trees are more widely spaced. The hills show more bare dirt. The distant fields have all been plowed and planted—to wheat, oats, barley, and corn, to pinto and horse beans, chick peas and potatoes, to garden plots of squashes and legumes. Where today the whole valley is in pasture and hay, then the only hayfields were lands too wet or stony to plow. And so the village, nestled in green mountains, dressed itself in brown: the brown of mud plaster on adobe homes, the brown of hills picked clean, the brown of bare earth waiting for the crops to rise.

Even by the age of ten, the boy who grew up feeding trees to goats and herding sheep on stingy hills had developed a sharp eye for what was useful. He had a disposition to gather, an instinct to leave nothing to waste. The sheep he herded could bear the winter healthily and well only if every salvageable scrap of fodder were put up for their use. The horses and cows, pigs and chickens, and by extension, the entire family, depended on this thoroughness. Silage, bran, and coarse grains were rationed through the winter. So were the *manojos* his father ordered him to make in autumn. After the main harvest, he and others went back and trimmed the edges of the fields. Any feed that could be cut and stored, was. And the judgment to do so was aesthetic as well as economic. A well-trimmed field pleased the eye. The scene appeared intact. *Manojos* looked good as you made them, and leaned them on the fence.

Field Canto

These hand-carved fields, worked by shovel, ax, and bar, don't want the water. Only the man does.

Take away the man, and the grass thickens in the ditch, the leaves catch, the silt settles out. Soon the water pools and leaks away.

Take away the man digging year by year, and all the ditches, large and small, swell with the surplus of the field's own growth. The ditch banks flatten under the weight of the hooves. The water spills out, useless.

Say good-bye then to the moist green sod. The broomstraw will take its place. Say good-bye to the mewing phoebe. The insect whine will retreat to the river.

Say good-bye also to the shy green snakes that the hawks love, and the splash from the hooves of the antic mare.

The field lives by the water but does not want it. The man lives by the field and makes it drink. He hears the suck of the sod as he deepens the ditch and the thwack of his shovel beating new clods in place.

"There now," he thinks. "That will hold a while." And he looks down the ditch at two hundred yards of clods undug.

He rests, and his fingers curl in a circle that fits the shaft of his shovel. He gazes upstream toward yesterday's ditch, and the ditches of days gone by—in this field, and that one, and the other through the trees. Fields and ditches that were made by hand.

Take away the man, and you take away the ditch.
Take away the ditch, and you take away the water.
Take away the water, and you take away the man.
You leave only the sound of the river.

7

The Society Is Losing
Our Mind

May 1976. The primary election is approaching. Anne takes Jacobo to Peñasco for groceries and horseshoe nails. At the filling station they meet Filiberto, who is nearly as old as Jacobo. With painful deliberation Filiberto is filling the tank of his pickup. The '53 Ford is well known in the area because Filiberto drives it so slowly that even the most nervous drivers must summon the courage to pass him. It has taken him half an hour to come the seven miles to Peñasco.

In Spanish Jacobo asks, "What are you doing here?"

"I came to hear the senator."

"But he is not here until tomorrow."

"But he speaks here today!"

"No he doesn't."

"I thought he did."

"Who told you that?"

"It was you who told me."

"I didn't tell you anything like that."

"Well."

"It's tomorrow."

"OK, tomorrow. You come with me?"

"Yes, got to be here at eleven."

"Eleven. OK, I pick you up at ten-thirty."

"Bueno, good-bye."

"Good-bye. See you."

Filiberto goes to pay for his gas. Jacobo turns to Anne, grinning, "He say he gonna see me . . ."

And Anne interrupts, "If you don't die and he don't go blind."

Jacobo looks blank, then grins more broadly, "That's right, *muchacha*. I can see you are learning something."

They wave to Filiberto as he turns his truck back toward El Valle. Anne waves as most people do, with a motion like washing a window. Jacobo waves in his own way: his hand upright, but rotating left and right, like the agitator of a washing machine.

Next morning Jacobo comes to the house early, as we are getting up. Alex, sleepy-eyed, lets him in, uttering a muffled, "Good morning, Jacobo." Jacobo regards him quizzically.

"You were still in bed?"

Then Anne enters the room. "Jacobo!" she says, "Come in. Come in." And takes his large hand in both of hers and leads him to the kitchen. Anne, like Alex, is from the South and surpasses even him for politeness. From my middle-Atlantic point of view, there seem to be times when a perverse, competitive urge seizes both of them and they thank and excuse and defer to one another as resolutely as though they were in combat. Next to them I generally feel rude, but sane.

Jacobo, being practical, delighted in Anne's solicitousness and constant attention. He quickly learned to use her generosity for all the pampering he could get, and she, recognizing deficiencies in certain of her housemates, seemed relieved to have found someone worth lavishing it on. Elsewhere, her openhearted kindness might have gone unappreciated, but in the village she became known as the *gringa pintora* whose hospitality equalled anyone's.

Anne guides the old man to a spot at the round table in the kitchen where the breakfast dishes have been cleared away.

Jacobo sits in a straight-back chair whose seat cushion has burst with cotton stuffing, and he spins the large lazy susan in the middle of the table. "I like this," he says to Anne as he continues to spin. "You don't have to ask for sugar, salt, anything, you just turn this thing and you take it."

Anne smiles. She knows his way of teasing.

A fifth of Jim Beam was left on the table from the night before. Jacobo spins the bottle within reach.

"Jacobo, would you like me to make you some coffee?" she asks.

"No, I'll just have some of this gin," he answers, seizing a tin measuring cup into which he pours two or three fingers of whiskey. "Anna."

"Yes, Jacobo?"

"You can be presiding judge for the primary," he says, giving Spanish pronunciation to the middle *i* in *presiding* so that it sounds like *preceding*.

"Excuse me?"

"But you got to go to school."

"What kind of judge?"

"Preceding judge. You will be in charge and so is Eremita, who is preceding judge for the Republicans." He explains that she will have to go to Taos to attend a session on how to operate the voting machine, what to do with voters whose names weren't on the precinct list, and how to file the records properly.

"Did you ever go to that class?" she asks him.

"Once, but learnt nothing, everybody talking in English. I won't go again unless they are going to speak Spanish."

Compensation for a twelve-hour day at the polling place was twenty-four dollars, which was good wages by our standards. Jacobo did his best to spread such jobs around, and most of the Democrats in the village appreciated his efforts. They also appreciated the fact that he kept for himself none of the campaign money the county Democratic Party gave him. Instead he redistributed it in the form of a dollar bill and one Schlitz beer to each Democrat who voted, at least until the beer ran out.

"Thank you, Jacobo." Anne says, and continues, meaning to compliment him. "You are a good . . . ," she fumbles for the right words.

He fills the gap: "good man!"

". . . precinct chairman."

"No, good man. I'm a good man, yes!" Jacobo downs his jolt of Beam, places the measuring cup on the lazy susan as he puckers and blinks, and spins it to the far side of the table. "I'm sorry. I got to go."

"Go where?"

"The senator is speaking." He pronounces it, *sen-A-tor*. "I got to get ready for U.S. Senator Montoya."

The meeting was at Tom's Place, a one-story adobe with a sagging roof. Years earlier, when the pastel green paint was fresh, Tom's had been a busy *sala de baile* and a focus of the town's social life. But that was before there were so many cars. Now the young people cruised from village to village, enjoying liquor in the comfort of their front seats, listening to tapes, talking to friends at the turnarounds. If they want to dance, they go to slicker dance halls in Española or Taos, or for a local party to the Acapulco in Vadito or to Peñasco's El Norteño, a steel warehouse of a dance hall with a bar on one side. Tom's Place, neglected by the young and vigorous, became a hangout mainly for hardcore drinkers from the town and Picuris Pueblo. Most nights, the drive-up window was Tom's only sign of life.

Back when Alex lived in Peñasco, we decided once to risk a beer at Tom's. We entered through a low door. The hall was chilly, cavernous, dark in the corners. Five men were at the bar, two of them very still, staring unfocused toward the bottles behind the bar. A burly sixth, with a puffy weathered face, staggered from the shadows and demanded our attention. He asked us if we would like to join him in a fight. There was no hostility in his invitation; it was strictly recreational, like asking someone to dance. We declined, and he polled the others at the bar, one by one. No one cared to accommodate him. But he kept asking, each of us in turn, and his syllables grew steadily furrier. The peaceful, gloomy melancholy of the bar became polluted with his garbled nagging. Finally a square-shouldered drinker two stools down from us stepped away from the bar. He looked the burly fellow over and launched a sober right cross that sent the big guy to the floor, presumably happier than when he had been standing. Alex and I drank up quickly and did not stay to see him awaken.

On the day of Senator Montoya's appearance, cars and pickups crowd the open roadside around Tom's Place. Bumper stickers and placards cover the front wall. Eager men in well-shined boots—the uncles, brothers-in-law, and drinking buddies of the candidates—press pamphlets into our hands as we go in.

It may be nearly midday outside, but the chronological reality inside Tom's is always a little past midnight. We pause for our eyes to adjust. The air is stale; there are no windows. What feeble light there is comes from three short fluorescent tubes spaced along the low crest of the ceiling, which is unpainted sheetrock, yellow with age, the nailheads and hammer dings showing. Crepe paper garlands of red, blue, and green swoop from the lights to the room corners. Whether they are newly installed or inherited from some past celebration is impossible in the dimness to determine.

The crowd numbers perhaps seventy people. Most of them stand in the back of the hall or lean against the side walls, which bear crude murals of imaginary landscapes. In one, vaqueros squat around a campfire; in another, ducks rise from a mountain lake. Tables and chairs have been dragged to the front of the hall, where the old men and a few women sit. We spot Jacobo and Filiberto, sitting very still, hats on the table before them, suffering their suits. Periodically others from the crowd, whom I don't recognize, squeeze through the chairs to shake their hands. Jacobo and Filiberto receive them as though they expected no less, nodding solemnly, and the visitors soon shuffle on again.

Beyond the old men, at the far end of the hall, a single high-wattage bulb hangs naked from its cord, as harsh as the sun, and under it, where the band ordinarily sets up, sits the man to whom Jacobo always refers by his full title: *U-S-Sen-A-tor-Montoya*. His suit, a celestial blue, the color of confidence and power, has just a hint of padding in the shoulders. The lapels lie flat and even, and no matter how he shifts or turns to receive the whispered reverences of those who buzz around him, the panels of the jacket hold their shape, a half-inch of cuff always showing. The senator's snowy hair and oiled face shine as brightly as the naked bulb. Even in the beery murk of Tom's Place, he seems sleek and imposing, like a Cadillac.

The senator has come to Peñasco to harvest the loyalty of the people the same way a forester takes timber neither he nor anyone else has planted. Crowding behind the senator are the dozen candidates for minor offices who hope to share that bounty with him. To the senator's left is his smartly dressed and ever-smiling wife, and to his right the Peñasco Democratic precinct chairman, in windbreaker and boots. Also at the speaker's table are State Senator C. B. Trujillo and sundry county incumbents. Ray García, the warm body being flung against Congressman Manuel Lujan in a hopeless race, leans against an upturned table in the darkest corner of the hall.

On the wall behind Montoya, in the glare of the light bulb, hangs a poster in English:

NOW—WHEN IT MATTERS MOST
SENATOR JOSEPH M.
MONTOYA
WORKS FOR ALL THE PEOPLE
RE-ELECT HIM NOV. 3

The sketch on the poster might be the senator. Or it might be a Kennedy or any smiling, strong-jawed, white-haired leader. Flanking it on either side are two small neon signs. One—in crimson—says, "A-1 Beer," the other, "Budweiser," in ozone blue script.

The program consists of a progression of minor candidates to a small space beside the senator's table where they speak into a handheld microphone. The loudspeaker to which the microphone leads lies on the table in front of the senator, aimed at the ceiling. Each candidate takes five or ten minutes to make his pitch before he yields to the next man, often his opponent.

Candidates for county clerk, treasurer, and assessor come and go; the nine prospective county commissioners, who are competing for three posts, begin to fidget, waiting their turns.

The audience is irreproachably polite. No conversations are whispered on the side, and except for one child asking loudly when the meeting will be over, there is no stray noise. The assembled Democrats listen respectfully and reward each speaker with a patter of applause. Jacobo, in particular, is rapt in his attention. His hands are calmly folded. He stares unwaveringly at the speaker. As precinct chairman for El Valle, he represents all the Democrats in the village, and he bears his duty with Jeffersonian diligence.

Except for U.S. Senator Montoya and State Senator Trujillo, the candidates are no different from their neighbors in the audience. None is a merchant or a businessman. All are farmers, small-scale ranchers, equipment operators, bus drivers, policemen, housewives. In recent weeks Jacobo has escorted many of them through the village, introducing them to every registered Democrat. To us they spoke a nervous, halting English (still far more fluent than our wretched Spanish), but inside Tom's Place, among *cuates y compadres*, all talk is in Spanish, and no gap exists between thought and word.

One man who cringed to speak English when he visited our home comes to the microphone and begins to shout, shaking his fist, stomping up and down. His Spanish is *puro norteño*—the contractions and colloquialisms, to say nothing of his intensity and rapid-fire delivery, leave me innocent of understanding. Certain of his words and verb forms are older than Goya would have used. He says *muncho* for *mucho* and *asina* for *así*, only *asina* is pronounced *a-HE-na*, for his *s*'s, along with *c*'s, *r*'s, and other letters I can't keep track of are aspirated like a *j*. There are times during his speech, it seems to me, when he omits more sounds than he actually makes. But that, as much as anything, is what marks me as an outsider. For anyone but a gringo, his speech is complete.

Later Jacobo explains that this most passionate of prospective county commissioners was promising, if elected, never to delegate clearing the snow from county roads to anyone else, but to get in the grader and do the job himself. His years as a heavy machinery operator, he said, were at the service of the people. The crowd received his harangue with much vigorous nodding of heads, and when he finished, the audience was wild in its appreciation.

Cleofes Vigil, a farmer, woodcarver, and singer of Penitente chants from north of Taos, is next to speak, and he too releases the emotions of the crowd. *"El Cristo era democrato,"* he proclaims with mock seriousness, and the room rocks with laughter. Vigil, a handsome, sturdy man, presses on, holding his hands in front of himself like a fighter. Christ was—and is—a Democrat, he explains, because he cares about the poor; His philosophy centers on the poor, and the Democratic Party, he sings out higher and louder, has always had a goal to *"creer en los pobres la misma filosofía del Cristo."*

Arms spread wide, opening himself to the audience, he confides that he entered politics, leaving his beloved ranchito, which he calls *"mi Monte Calvario,"* in order to bring sanity to government. Too many leaders are confused, he says, now switching to English. "Nobody is trusting anybody else, everyone is enemies, and what is happening is that the society is losing our mind. We don't work together anymore, and that is what I want to change. I want to work with people. I want good sanity in the way we run our county."

The applause for Cleofes has a happier ring than any that has preceded. U.S. Senator Montoya beams under the naked light. Perhaps no one takes Cleofes seriously, possibly not even the candidate himself, but no one says he isn't right. For the next several days Jacobo, for one, will recall his speech with a grin.

The procession of candidates continues. Each accepts the microphone with a bow toward the senator and the other dignitaries, then: *"Amigos y amigas, vecinos y vecinas, quiero piderles sus votos para. . . ."* None of the other speakers is as lively as Cleofes Vigil or as passionate as the grader operator, and as one speech blurs into another, the senator, who will attend a similar meeting in Questa at four o'clock and a third in Taos that evening, ceases to feign interest. He rubs his face with a soft, manicured hand, as though to wipe away not just the boredom but the slightly sticky film that descends on everything in Tom's Place. Within this dank cave of a building the light of the sun is only a memory, and the stale air seems to taste of headache and hangover.

Finally it is time to listen to Montoya. He rises at his chair. The microphone is brought to him. Beaming, wrinkle free, gold rings flashing on his fingers, he begins: *La gente del norte de Nuevo Mexico es mi gente. ¡Yo soy uno de ustedes!* I am one of you!

The man in impeccable board-of-directors clothes says to the people of Tom's Place: You are *mis primos*, my cousins, my friends who are so deeply held in my affection that you are like members of my family.

The senator's voice takes on an edge of anger and passion as he describes how racial discrimination lurks corruptively at the edges of the legislative process. But don't worry, he says, because he defeats it every time by writing affirmative action clauses in all the contracts for Los Alamos and Sandia Labs. He says that one day he hopes to bring federal jobs and money to Peñasco as he has to so many other parts of the state. His Republican opponents would never do as much. The Republicans never share his concern.

They are pouring money into New Mexico to defeat him, says the senator. The probable winner of the Republican primary, a former astronaut, is getting the biggest share of it because the big money interests from down south are behind him. The senator says he must ask the people of Peñasco once again for the help they have given so generously in the past. With their support, come election day, he will bury that astronaut, he says, pausing for effect—in a political graveyard on the moon!

The crowd applauds enthusiastically. The polite, attentive, and now happy faces in front of the senator are as wrinkled as old boots and just as weathered. The hairlines of their bristling crewcuts creep down their foreheads and the backs of their necks. The hands of the old men like Jacobo are the span of dinner plates and twisted with labor and age. Before them, in Tom's crepe-hung root cellar of a bar, U.S. Senator Montoya shines like a knight, and, at least for the moment, he is believed.

The Senator talks about his support of a ten percent increase in Social

Security benefits. More applause. He talks about hated communists and dictatorships—his Spanish loses me for a moment—but their evil is somehow connected to the Republicans and all the money they are spending to defeat Joe Montoya. "*¡Pero pesos no pueden comprar los amigos de Joe Montoya en el norte de Nuevo Mexico!*" Money can't buy the friends of Joe Montoya. He talks about federally financed college educations, about taxing the rich, about his humble boyhood in Peña Blanca.

He breathes deeply, almost sighs. "You know," he confides in a loud whisper, "people ask me why I pay so much attention to poor people, why I always try to work for them. And I answer them the same way Franklin Delano Roosevelt always answered that question: I say that I concern myself with the poor because there are so *many* of them!"

The senator sits. The crowd stands. The applause is loud and sustained. The senator wipes his face with a linen handkerchief, rises, bows. Well-wishers and favor seekers crowd toward him.

The meeting is over. Candidates troll the crowd, holding their hands at the ready for shaking. We see Jacobo making the rounds, working hard to keep his two canes and two legs separate from everybody else's. A lone drinker from Picuris wanders in, eyes glazed, fighting the current of the exiting crowd. We go out into the sunlight, taste fresh air again at last, its sweetness mingled with dust and oil smoke from the cars and pickups starting, pulling away.

Jacobo stands outside the door with Filiberto, like a minister after church. Everyone greets him. They call him Tío, Compadre, Primo, 'Mano, Cuate, every term of affection and respect. Many solicit his thoughts on the candidates and their speeches. We wait to speak with him, but the crowd around Jacobo only seems to grow larger. I hear him instruct the others, "We got to stand with Montoya, *y los otros candidatos. Esos republicanos* don't do nothing for us."

The clot of men at Tom's doorway has become an impromptu reunion of party loyalists from around the county. When we leave, the group is still animated, Jacobo at the center.

Later, in the afternoon, we ask Jacobo what he thought of the meeting.

"I like it fine. Everybody talk in Spanish. Not so good for you who speak only English, but the only good for me."

Next day a Montoya bumper sticker emblazons the door of his garage, facing the road. But Jacobo is not at home. Anne and I see him later at the far end of the village, astride the red horse. His mouth is puckered, the expression in his eyes serious as the giant horse plods on.

We stop the truck, roll down the window. "*¿Que pasa, Jacobo?*"

"*Estoy visitando los democratos,*" he says, "*casa por casa.* They got to know about the meeting, the candidates, and U.S. Senator Montoya."

8

The Body Politic

The afternoon following the Democratic meeting at Tom's Place, Jacobo visited Juan de Dios, Montoyita (even though he was Republican), José Isaac, and probably Epimenio. He also called on Filiberto, although Filiberto had attended the meeting, to discuss with Filiberto everyone else's reactions. He did not get to our house until the next morning.

He turned loose the red horse to eat weeds by the barn, and accepted the obligatory invitation to coffee.

I put on a pot, and Anne offered him a plate of fresh baked cookies called *bizcochitos*. Jacobo had made known his liking for them on other occasions, and these were thick and crisp, strongly flavored with anise. He helped himself to several but set them to the side.

"Jacobo, have a taste. Tell me if you like them," Anne said.

"Can't," he said. "Got to wait for the coffee."

"I thought you liked them."

"Yes, but I got to soak those *bizcochitos* in coffee to make them soft."

Anne had baked the *bizcochitos* mainly for Jacobo. "You don't like them the way they are?"

"I like 'em, but can't eat 'em," he explained. "I got no teeth."

"I know you've got none in the front, but none in the back either?"

"None. No way to chew if the food is hard."

"What happened?"

"Oh, they fall out," he shrugged, pursing his empty mouth. "Was a long time ago. They give too much trouble. I was glad to get rid of those teeth."

Anne was aghast, more at his attitude than his lack of teeth. Jacobo could hardly have been more pleased. "I got no way to smell, neither," he continued, playing the barbarian. "Was a time I come across a skunk, but I don't know it. The wife don't let me sleep in the house all summer. Only the porch for me." He grinned extra broadly, exposing his gums.

I poured coffee and Jacobo plunged a *bizcochito* into his cup. "These are good," he said, gumming furiously.

"Thanks, Jacobo," Anne said dryly.

Anne's tone jarred Jacobo to the realization that a man unable to distinguish between skunks and fresh air was less than credible on matters of flavor.

"Oh, but I can taste most things," he said, "especially sweet." He spun the lazy susan to bring the sugar bowl in reach, then ladled four spoonfuls into his coffee.

"You know," he said, "a friend in the sheeps told me your neighbor's sugar cannot be as sweet as your own. I guess that is true. That's why you got to use so much of it."

We smiled, not understanding the riddle but not wanting to appear stupid. It took a moment to appreciate how a person might covet a neighbor's sugar if his own supply—and cash to replenish it—were running so low that the sugar grew sweeter the scarcer it became.

The thought set Jacobo thinking about times past. Our conversations had a way of doing that, we being so different, so innocent of life before the *quebrada*, the break with the old days. Jacobo had come visiting that morning with politics in mind, and we talked briefly about the upcoming primary, about which candidates to back and which had the best chances. But soon the discussion turned to politics closer to home, politics rooted in the past.

In his younger days Jacobo had been fairly hot-tempered and combative. As a cook in a CCC camp during the depression, he took sufficient exception to a young Texan's comments about the food to attack the boy with a butcher knife. Fortunately for both of them, the gringo fled the mess tent and Jacobo drew no blood. At home in El Valle Jacobo's severest adversary had almost always been Efrén Chacón, who preceded him as Democratic precinct chairman and who, soon after the war, gave him the worst beating of his life.

Efrén served hard duty as a GI in World War II but otherwise, except "to follow the sheeps," rarely ventured beyond the confines of the village.

All his life he was the odd man out, the misfit who was never included in the plans or amusements of others. Efrén was a stutterer from early schooldays onward, and the children in the village, and not a few adults, mocked and taunted him. He grew up square-jawed, fit, and ramrod straight, the image of a soldier. He also grew up, soldier-like, to be a fighter, both to revenge himself against the ridicule he suffered and to defend his younger brother Elefio, who was less hardy and resilient than he, and Refugio, his spinster sister, both of whom were similarly outcast. There was a fourth sibling, Concepción, who eventually married Filiberto, but of the other three only Efrén ever came close to marriage. He became engaged—or thought he did—and built a house for his bride-to-be, high on the far side of the village in a broad stretch of sloping fields called the Llano de San Miguel. The saint's name, however, was dropped in general usage, and most people referred to the place simply as Llano Arriba, the high llano.

At the time of Efrén's engagement, Llano Arriba was home to eight or more families. They lived above the rest of the village, perched on a shoulder of the mountain ridge that enclosed the valley on the south. An earlier generation had cleared the llano of pines and sown the land to wheat and other grains. It was an altogether different environment from the rest of El Valle. Being so much higher, it seemed to abide in the embrace of towering Jicarilla Peak; it was much colder because the land lay open to the wind and sloped northward, turning its back on the winter sun, and more arduous because the road that led there climbed a shadowed canyon where snow piled in drifts and, melting, made the road a bath of mud.

But the view from Llano Arriba dazzled the eye. One could see over and beyond the valley walls. The great round mass of San Antonio Peak near the Colorado border anchored the northern horizon, and the long ridges of New Mexico's San Juan range faded to distant blues in the west. Directly below lay the houses, barns, and precise fields of El Valle itself.

In this splendid place Efrén Chacón labored, often alone, to make a trim adobe house with a corrugated roof and cleanly carpentered porch. He painted it green, with white and red trim on the porch posts, finishing it in time for the wedding. But there had been a misunderstanding. The bride said she had no wish to marry him, and no wedding took place. The clean new house smelling of plaster and paint now stank of heartbreak and humiliation. Efrén abandoned it, along with his hopes, and never moved in. The house has stood empty ever since, with doors locked and hearth cold, a monument to lonely sorrow.

Besides his brother and sisters, Efrén was nearly friendless. When it came time each year to harvest his hay, no one volunteered to help him. Elefio was too feeble to help and Efrén too cheap to hire an ordinary *peón*. So he would come looking for Alex and me.

It is a little known fact that gringos tend to look alike, and in the years we knew him Efrén never learned to tell us apart. Alex was Bill and Bill was Alex as often as either was himself. But Efrén was profuse in thanking us for the two or three loads of hay we hauled for him each year, and when Alex mentioned his interest in photography, Efrén genially invited him back to take as many pictures as he liked of Refugio, Elefio, and him. Once he even opened his wedding house and let Alex see the dusty emptiness inside.

Our contact with Efrén was noticed by Jacobo.

"Did he pay you for helping with the hay?"

"He offered but we said no thanks."

"That's why he offered," Jacobo said, "because he knew you don't take it."

"Maybe."

"And Elefio, *que estaba haciendo* while you bring the hay?"

"Watching, *no más*."

"He don't help?"

"We don't need him. Three were plenty: one to drive, two to load."

"Did you go in the house?"

"Yes."

"Refugio was there?"

"Yes, making posole."

And the interrogation continued until Jacobo was satisfied he had extracted every significant detail. He did not think badly of us for helping the man who was as much his enemy as any man in the world. On the contrary, our casual friendship with Efrén was useful to him. Jacobo was welcome in every other house in the village and thus kept current with the business of each family. Except the Chacóns. He observed them only at a distance, or through intermediaries like us, which was the more vexing because they mattered to him so.

The bad blood between Jacobo and Efrén started farther back than either could remember, but the lowest point in their history together came shortly after the war when Jacobo's brother, Amador, was elected to the county commission and held a victory dance at the school house. Efrén, who had supported another candidate, immediately began circulating a petition calling for Amador's removal from office on grounds of fraud, incompetence, and general bad character. As a result, no Chacón was welcome at the dance. But Elefio found the sounds of the party irresistible, and he hung around the schoolhouse, listening to the celebration.

As the evening progressed, Elefio did more than look in the windows. Someone reported to Jacobo that he was a nuisance to the men who were drinking outside and was making abusive comments about Amador and the entire Romero family. Jacobo decided to teach him a lesson.

He told the story many times: "I go outside and already Elefio is running away toward some barns that belong to Epimenio. Maybe he is looking for a stick to hit me. I go right after and hit him plenty on the shoulders and the head. I give him no chance to find the stick, no chance even to look at me because he got to keep his arms over his face or I gonna hit him there."

Jacobo backed Elefio up against a rail fence so Elefio could retreat no farther. He kneed him in the groin and kept punching until Elefio went down.

"Now he got no chance to get up and I am getting him pretty good—bloody mouth, bloody nose. So all he can do is reach for the fence and pull his head between the rails, and that is what happened. He got his head inside the corral and his body outside where I keep hitting."

Finally Jacobo let him up. Elefio scrambled to his feet and lurched into a run, only to slip as he jumped a small gully. He fell heavily in the mud and rocks, groaned, then scrambled up and fled into the safety of the night.

For the next hour the Romeros celebrated Jacobo's victory together with Amador's success in politics. Over and over, Jacobo recounted how he beat up Elefio, always ridiculing the way Elefio stuck his head through the fence, "like a cow that don't know where he is," and making fun of Elefio's clumsy, staggering escape.

The schoolhouse in those days had no electricity, and when one of the lamps ran low, Jacobo undertook to refill it with kerosene. Several friends stood by as he poured the oil, and they too kept reviewing the excitement of the night, relating to each other what slanders they'd heard against the Romeros and what they had seen of the fistfight. Suddenly Efrén burst through the door. Brass knuckles glinted on his right hand. His brother-in-law, Filiberto, followed him in along with one or two others and seized Jacobo from behind, yanking him to his feet. The lamp and the can of kerosene crashed to the floor, glass breaking, fuel splashing. The women screamed and ran for safety as the kerosene flooded across the floor toward the woodstove. Some ran out the door. Others made for the window. One girl dove through it head first, but not far enough. "She get stuck in the window, all her skirts up around her head and nothing to cover what is still in the room. You can see everything. For a little while she stays like that—what we call 'taking a picture.' She took a good one. Then she fall out."

It was the last picture Jacobo saw before Efrén's brass-knuckled fist began to crash into his face.

A man with a knife came to Jacobo's defense but was beaten down from behind. No one else dared take on the brass knuckles, and Efrén's allies let none of the men leave the room. When he finished with Jacobo, Efrén battered Amador. Finally satisfied, he wiped the blood from the brass knuckles, put them in his pocket, and soldier-straight, marched from the schoolhouse.

Having an enemy in a city or town is no guarantee of excitement. Unless circumstances repeatedly bring adversaries together, passions fade and the antagonists think of other things. Not so in a village. The cabin fever that accompanies close quarters and long winters can also occur at the scale of a community. People get on their neighbors' nerves and stay there because there is no way to escape—and so little else to do. The source of irritation lives nearby, he passes you on the road almost daily, his relatives treat your relatives coldly, you soon hear what he said about you at the store or the dance or in the socializing after church.

And you do not hesitate to reciprocate. Possibly you learn how to relish a fight, or the pleasure may have come to you naturally. Either way, you don't shy from it.

Jacobo eventually made friends with Filiberto—only after Filiberto had a falling out with Efrén that culminated in an all-out bruising fistfight from which Efrén emerged the victor. But Jacobo never made peace with Efrén. He talked about his run-ins with Efrén so often that it seemed the thought of him was never far from mind. His adversary embodied the things he disdained and disliked, things he had escaped. He was comfortable in the world outside the village. Efrén was not. He had a large, loving family; Efrén never married. He was a man to whom both words and friendships came easily; Efrén was the solitary stutterer. He had the regard of his neighbors, and they elected him Democratic precinct chairman; Efrén was the man he replaced.

Jacobo had been a Republican up to the mid-1960s, but the party did something to irritate him, or more particularly his brother Amador, and both of them switched parties. Jacobo was nominated and elected chairman at the first precinct meeting he attended. The only votes Efrén received were from Elefio and Refugio.

"So then I am chairman, but Efrén says to me that he will not have anything to do with me while I am chairman and for me not ever to nominate him to anything in his favor.

"But an election comes when we don't have many people to fill the positions, and I figure to see if Efrén still means what he said, so I put him down to be *alternate* election clerk. The clerk in Taos send him all the right instructions in English and Spanish, but Efrén still gets the idea he is to be *the* clerk who is to pass all the day of the election with the judges in the schoolhouse.

"Comes the election and he report for duty. The preceding judge give him the oath along with the others, but then he see there is one person too many. The judge ask me, 'Who is your clerk?' I say the name of the person who is clerk. Then the preceding judge tell Efrén that he will have to leave, and Efrén get plenty mad. He stomp on the floor and slam the door, but he has to leave. Then everybody laugh, and I notice that he never let go the ballpoint pen he took from the supplies when he thought he was the clerk. Seemed to me that was pretty good pay—to get a pen just for taking the oath."

Like precinct chairmen throughout the country, Jacobo's most important duty was to turn out the vote on election day. Since he had failed, decades earlier, to learn to drive a car, he sometimes hired me at a rate of five dollars a day, plus complimentary beers, to be his driver. Our electoral limousine was a yellow 1962 GMC pickup truck whose sides I'd caved in wrapping it around trees while hauling firewood on forest roads.

One of the voters we were obliged to fetch for the general election of 1976 was Onésimo Trujillo, then already past eighty. He was by far the best Democrat in the village, for he'd voted the straight party ticket in every election, never making exceptions, even for madmen and crooks. His was truly a blind loyalty, for he was entirely sightless. Although he was entitled to take someone into the voting booth to help him, he proudly refused to do so. Instead he entered the booth alone, felt the knobs and handles on the left side of the machine until he found the lever that tripped the entire democratic row, then cast all his votes with a single movement. That done, he yanked the big lever that opened the curtain and the Presiding Judge led him away.

As a young man, Onésimo had a reputation for being stern and difficult, but time and hardship eventually pulled the teeth of his meanness. He lived like a monk in a house near the head of the valley, rarely leaving the dim room in which he slept, except for elections and visits to the doctor.

Election day comes, and we go to fetch him shortly after lunch. His house is built on a west-facing knoll. It is one of the few two-story buildings in the village, and Onésimo not only roofed it with corrugated steel but sheathed the upper story with the same material. The shiny metal made his house a spectacle at sunset.

From where we lived at the opposite end of the valley, we watched the buildings and fields of the village turn warm and red with the last rays of the sun. And then, away in the distance, Onésimo's house seemed to ignite with silver fire, and we could hardly look away.

Jacobo says Onésimo married late in life and his wife died when his boys, Miguel and Ruben, were still little. He badly needed another wife to help take care of them but was himself no longer young. He sold half his land to some out-of-state gringos so he could move from the Llano Arriba and build a house on the warmer side of the valley. He hoped that the new house and the cash he had left would compensate for his age and help him attract a wife.

But the boys were wild and no woman wished to take them on. Onésimo struggled alone. As they grew older, the boys' rebellion grew worse. Miguel, the older of the two, led Ruben in making life hellish for their father. Ultimately, Onésimo drove them away, virtually at the point of a gun. They went to work in the mines in Leadville.

Years later, Onésimo was blinded by a battery that exploded when he tried to jump-start the tractor from his pickup. The money from the land was gone, and he had not found a wife. He had to sell his cattle to pay for medical expenses and a housekeeper. Pretty soon he had no income but the meager rent his remaining fields produced.

He pleaded with his boys to come back, but they did not answer his letters. Miguel, the elder of the two, was too proud and too bitter. Already a foreman at the mine, he had a company truck and a job that kept him above ground most of the time. Ruben was also making good money. Miguel pulled strings and got him a job topside, in the sun, and he was well set up. He married, bought a used Cadillac, and bragged that he too would make foreman soon.

But Ruben smoldered. Without a word to Miguel, he persuaded his father to sign over the deed to the house and all the land that had not been sold to the gringos, leaving none for his brother. Miguel knew nothing of their pact until Ruben quit his job at the mine and left Leadville. Later it dawned on him, as it did on Jacobo, that, as much as Ruben hated his father for selling the land and throwing him out, he hated his brother for enlisting him in the destruction of his family.

When Jacobo and I arrive at Onésimo's house, three shepherd dogs race snarling to the truck, lips back, teeth wet. Jacobo gets out and swings at them with a cane. Two retreat to the swing set Ruben's children use. The third takes cover behind a discarded engine block and glowers at me. I hear the sound of a TV soap opera coming from the second floor. I can see Jacobo's house a mile to the northwest, and the giant cottonwood that shades it.

Ruben and his family live in the upstairs rooms, which connect by a balcony. The downstairs is used for storage and Onésimo. Jacobo knocks on a door and a faint voice bids us enter. The old man's dim blue room contains a wrought iron bed, a woodstove, and a ladder-back chair. Onésimo sits in the chair with his hands on his cane, chin on his hands. A small table bears the remnants of a breakfast that Ruben's wife has not yet cleared away. She keeps a flashlight by the door because Onésimo never let them wire the room. He was already blind when power lines reached the village, and he told Ruben that he would not pay for light he could not see.

I stand at the door while Jacobo talks to the old man. The turquoise walls have a handcarved look, as though the plaster had been daubed and smoothed without the help of tools. There is an ancient photograph of Onésimo's wife on the washstand in the corner and a picture of the Last Supper over the bed. The room smells faintly of lemon soap.

Onésimo used to be a big man, and his long-limbed frame dwarfs the spindly chair he sits in. His milky eyes stare into the shadows as Jacobo relates the news from the schoolhouse: who has come to vote, what if anything the voters talked about. When Onésimo speaks, his voice sounds tentative, almost painful, like the creak of unused machinery. Although the words are deliberate and clear, the sentences are strangely elliptic, and I cannot follow their meaning. Even another *anciano* like Jacobo cannot always understand what the old man is trying to say, and so when Onésimo tells us that it is not yet time for him to vote and that we had better come back at sundown, we ask no further questions and politely take our leave.

We return to the schoolhouse, which has not seen a class of students since the Peñasco Valley schools were consolidated more than a decade ago. Now the building is used only as a polling place and for parties and meetings of the ditch associations. As a result it is badly out of repair, with sparrows nesting in the cupola where the bell hangs and sheets of metal roofing coming loose and creaking in the wind.

Ruben is there; his bushy eyebrows and long flat cheeks give him a frowning look. Jacobo greets him with diffident good humor. Ruben is standing in for the Republican Precinct Chairman, who is sick. It is a post that exists more in name than in duty, at least in Jacobo's view, since "the Republicans don't listen to anybody, especially Ruben."

The Democrats, on the other hand, are active and organized, and no doubt the dollar bills and beers that Jacobo dispenses contribute to political solidarity. Good manners require that we give a Democratic beer to Ruben, and we sip ours and gossip with the judges and clerks, Anne among them, who have come out of the schoolhouse since the last voter left an hour ago. Election days are always slow. Twelve hours to keep the polls open for a turnout of forty-four voters. Anne says they have talked

all they can about the weather and everyone's children, and now they are
just watching the clock.

Ruben says the gringos are giving him trouble again. He says they have not visited the property in years and the walls of the irrigation ditch that waters it are breaking in many places. "I write them letters, but they don't answer."

"But your cattle eat the grass there," says Jacobo. "Why don't you fix it?"

"*Pero* you don't know how much work is there. I need money to bring a backhoe." The long dour face cracks into a smile, "Unless you want to rent it this summer, then you can see how that ditch leaks."

"Yah, we got too many leaks in this valley. Maybe more leaks than shovels," says Jacobo. "Maybe as many as politicians, *que no*? So now we can vote to get rid of some of them."

Ruben resumes his frown. The judges and clerks talk about how sleepy it makes them to sit inside all day.

At last the sun gets low and red, and we head up the road to get Onésimo. The flat light of sunset has kindled its fire on the sheet metal of the old man's house, but as we turn into his drive and the shepherd dogs commence their vicious show, our angle changes and the fire seems to dim and go out. Onésimo is still in his chair, only now the sunlight streams under the balcony, through his door, and strikes him full in the face. He is bathed in the strong red light so that even his smoky eyes seem to capture a spark.

"Are you ready?" Jacobo asks.

Almost imperceptibly, he shakes his head. And so we wait, and in the fading light his face wears a calm I have never seen before, the cheeks and forehead utterly slack, skin bleached with scarring, eyes the color of chalk, mouth open and breath faint, each whisker stiff and gray and casting a tiny shadow against his chin.

The bottom of the sun touches a distant mountain and we feel its intensity die. The roof creaks loudly, contracting. Onésimo says, "*Bueno, estoy listo.*" I am ready.

Jacobo carefully leads him outside to the yellow truck, and we guide him to the seat, lifting him gently and taking care lest his head hit the door frame, folding his great long limbs to fit within the cab. Onésimo suffers the indignity of this packaging with stony silence, revealing nothing of how he feels at being unearthed from his room and carried into the world.

Ruben is still at the schoolhouse when we get back. It is nearly dark, but the air is pleasant, warm for November, and everyone is standing outside. I turn off the engine, and Jacobo guides Onésimo's feet toward the ground. The blind man probes the ground with his cane. Several steps from the truck, he pauses, and stretches up to full height. Then, not waiting for Jacobo to take his arm, he starts forward toward the voices that are gathered by the schoolhouse door. Jacobo presents him formally to each person, some of whom Onésimo knows, some he has forgotten, others he has never met. He takes the hand and repeats the name of each, bowing in an old fashioned way, until he comes to Anne, whom Jacobo introduces as a teacher from the high school, Anne McLaughlin. At the sound of so foreign a name, Onésimo smiles slightly, and surprises all of us by saying stiffly, in English, "I am pleased to meet you, my dear lady."

His smile stays with him until he reaches the door of the schoolhouse, and Ruben. Jacobo says, "And here is your son."

For the first time since his arrival at the schoolhouse a crowded, feeble-minded look comes over him. "Are you the son of old Onésimo?" he asks.

"Yes, I am Ruben, papa."

"Well you must visit me, then. My son Miguel comes to visit all the time."

Ruben let go of his father's hand, and the two turned away from each other slowly, symmetrically, like dancers. The presiding judge took Onésimo's arm and led him into the schoolhouse, the clerks and other judges following, and they gave the old man a paper on which he stiffly, with crooked lines, made his mark: a cross imposed upon a circle.

Then the presiding judge led him to the voting booth, where Onésimo gave each Democratic candidate, without exception, one vote more.

9

Red Horse

Most years in September, after the hay is put up and the branches of the apple trees sag with fruit, the unsettled afternoons of summer give way to cloudless, high-pressure skies. For weeks on end the weather stays dry and clear. When time avails, we busy ourselves hauling truckloads of firewood from the forest. Chain saws rasp through the valley from morning to night, as we and our neighbors cut the wood to length and stack the blocks for winter splitting. Robins gather in ever larger flocks, and *piñoneros* (Clark's nutcrackers) fly up and down the ridges, their crops full of newly ripened piñon nuts, which they cache in the high country. The aspen, then the cottonwoods by the river turn gold, and the roadside grasses cure out, together with the chamisa and wildflowers, drying stiff, brittle, and every shade from chestnut to rust.

But some years, the smooth progression of seasons stalls. A tropical storm, born over the Gulf of Mexico, strays across the plains and lodges on the peaks, bringing days of heavy rain. Our land was suited to hard winters and dry summers. Such trials were part of the land itself. It was rain, abundant rain, that rendered us most vulnerable and pushed both land and people past their limits.

One September, a change in the weather caused restlessness among us all. I wrote in my journal, "Anne is depressed and cannot sleep. Neither can I. We stare at patterns on the wall. Light comes from Tomás's security lamp and passes through the leaves of an elm outside our window. A wind has risen and stirs the tree. Its shadows dance wildly, malevolently, in our room."

In the morning we found one of our chickens dying in the coop. Not knowing what ailed it, we put the sick bird in a storeroom, separate from the others.

That afternoon the storm broke.

It rained through the night and all the next day. We stayed in, not talking much, feeling as gray as the weather. Toward sundown of the second day the storm eased to a drizzle, and I took the opportunity to move my horse from the house corral down to pasture. In a grocery bag I carried the now dead chicken, which I meant to discard far from the house on account of our dogs. They would live longer, I figured, if they never learned the taste of a bird, dead or alive, healthy or sick.

But someone let them out of the shed where I locked them, and they caught up to me as I was about to pitch the bird into an arroyo. I walked a short way into the forest and wedged the chicken, out of reach, in a tree. Ravens and magpies would do the rest.

Drizzle pattered on the leaves of ditchside alders and willows as I followed the muddy road homeward. There were no cars on the road, and in the first quarter-mile, no house lights in the distance. The waning sun reflected weakly in the road puddles, and except for the rain and the wet snuffling of the dogs along the road edge, all was silent. Then, as I passed the gate to one of Jacobo's pastures, I heard a groan.

It was a small pasture, and appeared empty. The groan sounded again, low and piteous. Followed by a splash.

I opened the gate and rounded some alders that arched above the *acequia*. Another splash and a grunt. The bank of the ditch was high, built up with stumps and stones from years of repair. At a bend of the ditch where the trees opened, a great head rose from the liquid darkness, eyes wide with fright, nostrils flared. It was Jacobo's red horse.

The horse neighed in recognition, then groaned and lunged to get up, but fell back heavily. Cold black water dammed against its breast and swirled over its shoulders. In the darkness I saw only its head and a single front hoof that scratched at the ditchbank.

I hurried to Jacobo's house. Liza was washing the dinner plates. He was drinking coffee.

"Jacobo," I said, "I have bad news. Your horse has fallen in the ditch and can't get up. It looks bad."

"Where?"

"One fence down. In the little pasture before the arroyo." Wordlessly,

Liza dried her hands with a towel. Her eyes were on Jacobo. He had risen from his chair and leaned for a moment, both hands on the chair back, staring at the floor.

I said, "Maybe he is only pinned there by some branches. But maybe he is crippled."

"Let's go see," he said and took a large electric lantern from atop the refrigerator. On the porch he sat down to put on his rubber boots.

I remembered the ditch. "We need to put the water out," I said. "What gate should I use?"

"Use that one by the *alamo*. You can put it all there."

When I came back from the water gate, he wore a yellow slicker and held, besides the electric lantern, a frayed halter and a lead rope. "*La vieja* called Tomás," he said. "We gonna need more help."

The drizzle had grown to a shower that drummed on the roof. My denim jacket was soaked. "I need a dry coat," I said. "I'll get Alex and meet you by the horse."

At the house Alex, Anne, and I put on hats, gloves, ponchos, boots. I noticed the clock read a quarter past seven. Little was said, or needed to be. If the horse were crippled, it would have to die.

Tomás was already in the pasture when we got there, his pickup parked with engine running so that its headlights shone into the tunnel of trees that concealed the horse. The yellow cones of light were filled with falling rain and mist steaming from the truck hood.

We could see the horse and, incompletely, its predicament. Its eyes were small moons, sightless from terror and the glare of headlights. Already its efforts to lunge free seemed less vigorous than before. Between lunges the horse laid its head on the weedy edge of the ditch and rolled its giant eyes.

Although the flow was cut, water still pooled around the horse's shoulders and hips, obscuring the angle of its legs. The best we could determine was that the forelegs were free and the damage was in the hindquarters, but we could not be sure. A stout juniper angled from the ditchbank, and thick foliage shrouded everything the water might otherwise have let us see. The horse lay beneath the horizontal trunk of the juniper, possibly trapped by it, and alders crowded from the other side.

Tomás called for a chain saw, and Jacobo explained to Alex where it lay in the toolroom. "Get the *vieja* if you can't find it. She knows where."

Alex disappeared into the darkness, and Jacobo strode forward, halter in hand. He bent toward the horse, opening the halter, and suddenly the horse lunged again with a violent splash, one great round hoof erupting from the water and stabbing the ditchbank. Jacobo staggered stiffly backward. Small gobs of mud stained his face.

Tomás took the halter from Jacobo and edged toward the horse, murmuring softly. However crippled the horse might be, it could still give serious injury if one failed to stay clear of its hooves and head. There was little Jacobo could do. He watched intently and silently, his face frozen in a scowl, as Tomás dodged several, less violent lunges and at last fitted the halter on the horse and buckled it tight.

Tomás clipped the lead rope to the halter and all of us pulled together. The horse's head and neck stretched out, as though in supplication, and the beast thrashed vainly with its forelegs. It rose a few inches and no more. We eased the rope and the horse settled back into the water, groaning until its lungs were empty.

"Maybe those branches hold him back." Tomás said. "We better wait for the *serruche*."

"Yah," Jacobo agreed, but not with much conviction. "With the chain saw maybe we get him out."

The rain beat down, and the truck engine growled. We stared where the headlights blazed on the horse and the trees. Flashlight in hand, Anne searched the thicket behind the horse. Her green, hooded poncho, drawstring tight around her face, glistened in the light. "I thought the horse maybe backed into the trees to get out of the rain. Then slipped where it was slick, and fell into the ditch. But I can't find where he went in, or the tracks where he slipped."

She handed Tomás the flashlight and he cast its beam quickly over the same ground where she had looked. "No. Probably we can't figure out how that horse got in there." The rain ran off the brim of his Resistol in a steady stream. "Crazy horse," he muttered, which was how he described any horse—or cow or pickup truck—that misbehaved or broke down. In a rare concession to solemnity he did not say the second half of his refrain, but we all felt him think it: "Crazy horse—just like the owner." Even Jacobo broke his meditation and cast Tomás half a smile.

Tomás was the biggest man in the village—or for that matter for several villages around. He stood a half head taller than I, and I break six feet.

His girth in the chest and shoulders, and no less in the gut, was monumental. One could not be unaware of his strength. Nor could one miss his presence in village affairs, for nothing occurred without his involvement. He drove the school bus, ran a small store and service station, and managed two dozen head of cattle. Since the last election, he also served as deputy sheriff, and had a badge, a .357, and a siren on his truck to prove it. And he was *mayordomo* of our ditch.

It was Tomás who had sold me my horse. When I bought it, I thought it was a beautiful animal, but in time the infatuation of first ownership wore off, and I was obliged to appreciate its considerable ugliness. It had a roman nose, feet as big as frying pans, and a lower lip like a bicycle tire. Bareback, its withers would threaten your genetic future. Fortunately, it was also strong and virtually indestructible, which saved it from my recklessness, and also, considering the spills we took, may have saved me from myself. The horse had no affection for humans, however, and ran off whenever it could. Once I lost it in deep forest far from home when I dismounted to catch a stray calf of Tomás's. The next day I found the horse, stripped of saddle, bridle, and pad, outside Pacheco's bar in Truchas. Tomás generously helped me find a new saddle and bargained a good price for it, but he lectured me long and loud not to let it happen again. "Don't trust 'em!" he almost shouted. "Every horse, *every horse!*" he ranted as though I were hard of hearing, "is a crook son of a bitch!"

I halfway wished it were my crook son of a bitch lying in the ditch, instead of Jacobo's. There were other horses I could ride, but none for Jacobo. No other horse would hold so still or pace the road so dreamily, as befitted both the old man's safety and his dignity. The red horse was older than I and nearly half as old as Jacobo. Now it lay in numbing waters, its back quite likely broken, or its pelvis, or one or both hind legs. There was only the slightest possibility that the canted trunk of the juniper was all that kept it from rising, but we clung to that hope, at least in what we said. I, for one, clung to it partly for fear of what we might do, if once the trunk were cut, the horse did not rise.

At last Alex returned with a yellow McCullough. Tomás yanked the starter cord, and the saw rattled and then was silent. He fiddled with the choke and the gas trigger, and yanked the cord three times more, and the yellow saw roared to life.

The horse lay with its head against the bank, and as Tomás approached with the growling saw, the one eye we could see widened to the size of a baseball. Tomás commenced to cut the alders behind the horse's head. The saw rasped through the narrow trunks, and I caught the trees to keep them from falling on the horse. But the panicked eye unnerved me. It stared as though it expected me to pierce it with a jagged, new-cut sapling. And I, slipping in the wet and struggling to stay clear of both horse and saw, half-feared I might.

Tomás finished with the alders and started on the juniper. Alex and I steadied the tree by its branches while he topped it. The wet chips sprayed over the horse, adding a cedar smell to the oily exhaust of the saw. I kept an eye on the horse, in case he lunged, and watched great shivers ripple through the red-haired hide.

The top of the juniper came free, branches whipping a spray of rainwater, and we pushed it as it fell, toppling it into the pasture. Tomás shut off the saw, and there was quiet. Behind the low roar of the truck engine, we felt the finality of the night.

Now at last the canopy was open and we craned, flashlights and lanterns in hand, to see how the horse lay. Its volume nearly filled the ditch. I was relieved to see no sign of blood in the water that pooled around it. At least, I thought, the horse is not impaled on a stub. But what we most needed to see was still concealed. The horse's hind legs lay crammed into a cavity where ditch water had undercut the bank. I could not tell if the legs were free or trapped in roots. There was doubt on the faces of the others, too.

"*¿Que dices, Jacobo?*" Tomás finally asked. "*¿Que quieres hacer?*"

"She don't look cripple that I can tell. We can cut the rest of that cedar and see can she get up."

Tomás cranked the McCullough, revving loudly until it ran smooth. Jacobo watched from the edge of our field of light, his hat soaked, face wet, features solemn.

The canted juniper lay across the horse's shoulder, and where Tomás would cut it, horseflesh was separate from wood by a gap of an inch, maybe two. Tomás kneeled in the mud of the ditchbank and began to cut. The horse recoiled, eyes bulging, nostrils flared, and strained away from the snarling saw.

The saw bit into the wood, flashing sparks where it struck bits of gravel in the bark. The wood was hard, the chain dull, and smoke and steam rose from the kerf. A stripe of sawdust and black chain oil spat out across the shoulder of the horse. I stood on the bank and leaned above the horse to hold the stump from binding or falling. The saw screamed at full throttle. I looked at Jacobo at the edge of the light. His toothless jaws were clenched.

The horse no doubt felt the heat of the saw and the wind of its whirring chain. It shuddered without stopping, and its tremors grew wilder and more violent. I feared that it might convulse into the path of the teeth.

But Tomás never wavered. His big hands pressed the saw to its work, and at last I felt the trunk take on weight and lean from the stump. It came free in my hand and I lobbed it into the darkness. Tomás killed the saw. Each of us stepped back and took a breath together. We did not speak but stood listening to the tremulous panting of the horse, which now quaked louder than the rumble of the truck.

"*A ver*, Jacobo," said Tomás, "let's see now."

Wordlessly Jacobo picked the end of the lead rope out of the mud. The horse shook its head as the old man began to pull.

Tomás also took hold and pulled together with Jacobo. The horse laid back his ears, eyes wide, and groaned as the men put their weight to the rope. The horse's front hooves clawed the bank as it sought to right itself and move its weight atop its legs. But the horse's strength was gone, and its hindquarters did not budge. The horse sank back against the rope, staring at us.

Jacobo and Tomás tried several times more to force the horse to rise, as Alex and I looked on. After the first effort, Anne touched me on the arm and whispered she was leaving. There was no more help to give or hope to keep. Her green poncho faded into darkness as she climbed the track to the pasture gate, and I heard her steps go by above us on the road.

Tomás let go of the rope and turned to the old man. "Jacobo, that horse can't get out of the ditch by himself."

"Well, go and get the tractor then," the old man said, and he did not turn to watch Tomás climb into the truck, slam the door, and pull out into the pasture. We heard the wheels spin wetly as Tomás gunned the truck toward the gate. For a moment it seemed he might not make it up the slick grade to the road, and I realized I hoped he would not, but at last he gained the top and roared toward the station.

Night reclaimed us. Without the glare of headlights on the mired horse, we were each alone, without focus. We stood separate from each other, wanting to speak but finding no words that did not sound like defeat. The horse lay still. Its sides heaved but less violently than before. The wet rails of the pasture fence gleamed behind us. The rain droned.

"Jacobo, let's go wait for Tomás on your porch," Alex said. "We don't need to stay in the rain."

"No, it don't take much time to drive the tractor here. We can wait."

And so we waited, feeling the cold and wet leak through the shoulders of our jackets. Like dull sentries we shifted weight from foot to foot, our attention given more to shivering than duty. Only Jacobo stood immobile. He made no effort to touch or stroke the stricken horse and offered it no words of reassurance, but he would not leave it. In the dark the lines of his face seemed deeper than in daylight, and more rigid.

I worried how the horse might suffer when the tractor did its work. "Jacobo, do you think one of his legs might be caught by roots?" I asked.

"Could be. We gonna see."

"It could break his leg."

We were standing now face to face, and I could see beads of rainwater in the stubble of his whiskers. His gaze was like a too-strong handshake, firm but not his own.

"Bill, we got no choice," he said.

"We could wait until morning, when we can see better."

"Then he gonna die from the water and the cold. No. We got to pull him out."

We turned back to stare into the darkness where the horse lay.

Minutes later we heard the low-geared grinding of Tomás's tractor. It approached slowly, the drone scarcely seeming to change, but when the tractor finally turned through the pasture gate, its roaring filled our ears and drove away the insulating solitude we'd felt. The weak twin beams of its headlights swung around to find us, glum and dripping, by the ditch.

Tomás's tractor was an old John Deere with an open seat and four-foot tires in the rear. It was familiar to all of us, for we depended on Tomás to bale our hay, plow and grade our roads, and pull our trucks from the mud holes we stuck them in. Now he backed it to the ditch, awakening the horse from the numbness of injury and cold, and again we saw the big eyes swell with panic.

Tomás reached into a cargo box beneath the tractor seat and removed a long steel chain with links like giant bracelets. He threw one end over the shoulder of the horse and told us to haul on the lead rope. As we pulled, he lay down in the mud of the ditchbank and reached under the horse's chest for the end of the chain. We pulled with all our might and the horse rose up just far enough for Tomás to pull the chain through. He closed the loop by hooking the chain to itself and secured the other end to the tractor. We then unsnapped the lead rope from the halter and looped it around the horse's forelegs, one at a time, to lift and hold them clear of the ditch bank so that they, at least, would be safe from further injury.

It might have been better to pull the horse out of the ditch by the path that led him in, but as Jacobo said, we had no choice. Even if we knew how the horse had fallen, neither the trees, the twisting of the ditch, nor the anatomy of the horse would have permitted it. Tomás climbed onto the tractor and released the hand brake. The chain grew taut. I pulled the forelegs up to clear the ditch bank, then walked away fast to put the sound of the tractor between me and the sound of the horse.

The tractor roared. I heard desperate groans. There was the sound of popping and cracking, but it may have been only the underbrush.

I looked back and saw the horse, its head lolling against the chain, dragged slowly and limply across the pasture grass.

We unhitched the chain from the tractor, and Tomás turned the machine to shine its lights upon the horse. Its hide showed several bleeding wounds, but nothing serious. The legs looked straight enough, no grievous angles. I thought we should have let the horse rest, but Jacobo impatiently clipped the lead rope to the halter.

He yanked on it. "Get up, you son of a bitchy. Get up!"

The horse neither sought to rise nor pulled back against the rope. It had no heart to move, and likely not the ability. Its eyes were empty even of fear.

"Let's turn him over," said Tomás, and together we levered him over by the legs and pulled the chain free. Again Jacobo tried to yank him to his feet, but the result was the same. The horse would not move.

Tomás put the chain in the cargo box of the tractor and swung into the seat. "We can't do no more tonight, Jacobo. Maybe he can get up in the morning, after he rests."

"Yah, maybe." His voice had no conviction, but he stood a moment silently considering the prospects, toothless gums working. Then he

pulled off a sodden glove and thrust out his hand to Tomás. "*Pues, gracias.*
Thank you very much, Tomás. We gonna see in the morning how he is."
Jacobo turned from the rest of us and started toward the gate. "I got to get
some hay," he muttered, "to cover him with." Alex followed him out of
the pasture.

Tomás fired up the tractor. Speaking just above the sound of the
engine, he said to me, "We have to kill that horse tomorrow."

"Yes," I said. "Too bad. Jacobo can't find a horse like that again."

"No, he is an old man. No more *caballero* for him." The transmission
clanked as Tomás put the tractor in gear and steered toward the gate.

I waited by the quiet horse until Jacobo and Alex returned with the
hay, Jacobo in front, on his canes, Alex following and dragging a fresh
green bale by a hook. We fluffed the hay and spread it over the horse to
warm him, covering all but the head, and Jacobo picked out handfuls of
alfalfa from the bale and laid them by the horse's mouth. In silence we
trudged back to Jacobo's house, bid the old man goodnight, and continued home. We threw our wet clothes in a heap on the floor, and dirty
and damp, crawled into our beds. It was midnight.

By morning the weather had broken, and the sun raised a cool mist
from the fields. We debated when to call on Jacobo and agreed to put it off
for several hours.

We got no work done. I interrupted Alex in his darkroom. He was
sorting prints, nothing important.

"Well?"

"Well, at least it wasn't a pet," he said. "Anyway he never gave a sign
that it was."

"No, no more than a horse. But maybe he feels more than he shows."

"It's like an amputation. It saws him off, cuts him back to ordinary legs,
which don't work very well."

"Cuts him back to being just an old man. Now he'll be dependent, just
to get around, to see his friends."

"He'll be in the same shape as they are."

"He hasn't had to see himself that way."

"Until now."

"No."

"Think he'll give up? Some of them have given up."

"Might. I might if I were him."

The sun was high when Alex and I walked down the road, past Jacobo's house, to the pasture where the horse lay. Jacobo had been there. He'd swept away the hay that covered the horse so that the heat of the sun could touch its skin, and he'd put a bucket of water near its mouth. But there was no sign the horse had moved, and it did not budge or nicker when we approached.

There were black ruts where the tractor had torn the pasture sod and a path of flattened grass where the horse had dragged. We saw the ragged hole in the canopy along the ditch where we had labored, and around it lay juniper boughs and leafy alder stems, already wilting in the warmth of the day.

We walked back up the road and found Jacobo on his porch, sitting in profile to us, eyes straight ahead, expression neutral. He did not rise from his truck seat couch as he usually did when we opened the picket gate. He raised a hand in silent greeting and continued staring in the direction of the ditch, the fields, the valley. We pulled up chairs and stared the same as he.

"The horse doesn't get up," I say.

"No, he don't."

"We gonna have to shoot him?"

"I guess. If he don't get up." Jacobo worked his jaws, then spoke again. "I can't shoot him," he said.

There was a silence. Then he added, "Can't hold the rifle steady no more." And he held one of his canes to his shoulder, hands shaking, the point of the cane dancing in exaggerated circles. He put the cane down. "And anyhow, I can't shoot that horse."

"We can shoot him for you."

"You can shoot him?"

"Yeah, but we've got no gun."

"I got a gun."

"When do you want us to shoot him?"

"Not today. I gonna give him one more day."

"One more day?"

"Yah, one more day. To see if he get up."

"All right."

"Maybe he will get up tomorrow."

"Maybe."

"We can see in the morning."

"OK. See you tomorrow."

"Yah, tomorrow."

Our boots sounded hollow against the planks of the porch as we walked back to the gate. Liza came to the kitchen door. She greeted us softly and leaned out to peer at Jacobo. Evidently she was keeping a close eye on him. We told her we were sad for the horse and for Jacobo. She shrugged, raising her hands emptily. It was a gesture of lament she'd had occasion to practice many times in her seventy-three years. "Yes," she said, "it is hard for Jacobo, but nothing we can do."

Next morning we went first to the pasture where the horse lay. We didn't go in. We could see from the road that nothing had changed.

We went to Jacobo's.

The rifle leaned against the wall, just inside the picket gate. Jacobo sat on the truck seat in the same posture as the day before.

"Shall we go ahead, Jacobo?"

"Go ahead."

Alex picked up the rifle, and we started down the road. There were three shells in it. A month earlier Alex had hunted caribou in Alaska. By his look, he intended to do the shooting. It was no task I cared to claim for myself, and we did not discuss it.

We entered the pasture and approached the horse, which lay facing us, watching us closely. At twenty feet, Alex stopped and raised the rifle. The horse lifted its head slightly, to see us with both its eyes. The report of the gun rocketed through the valley.

We left the rifle on the porch where we had found it. Jacobo was not there.

Later that afternoon, Tomás brought his tractor, and I helped him hitch a chain to a hind leg and drag the carcass out of the pasture, across the road, and up a broad arroyo. We left it amid a litter of bleaching ribs and skulls, in a place where butchered animals were cast away.

Hours later, vultures funneled above the ridge.

10

Gringismo

Alex never photographed the red horse, and the red horse never had a name. Like much else in the history of small places, the horse epitomized something basic about the land that nourished it. It was an embodiment, literally, of the valley's grass and water, and a relic of its weather. Living, it had been a definition of local horseness, ridden by an old man and plodding as slowly as the change of seasons down the dusty village road. The red horse passed its years, stalwart and unique, then dropped from sight, and eventually will drop from memory too, as slowly, without it, the place changes.

Alex never photographed the horse because it took him time, as it did me, to awaken to the possibilities of what might be done so close to home, what kind of partnership might be struck with Jacobo. Alex was focused elsewhere. At the time of the red horse's death, he still traveled once or twice a year to Alaska. When he was home, he labored in the darkroom, wrote grant applications, and occasionally went east to give a lecture or teach a course. The red horse was a subject he'd attend to when time permitted. Time never did. And regret took root where satisfaction might have been.

The horse had no name because Jacobo saw no utility in naming it. To Jacobo, its value was instrumental, not intrinsic. The horse existed to serve him and could serve namelessly. While the horse may have viewed its purpose in life differently, namelessness seemed to suit it. The truest horses, wild ones, lacked names too. And the red horse had been all horse, not an ounce of Flicka.

Still, the lack of a name made the horse no easier for the old man to forget. No one, grown weak, forgets what it was like to have strength. No one who loses a limb forgets how it felt to be whole.

The virtue of namelessness was that it made the unforgettable easier to avoid. Jacobo never mentioned the red horse. Nor did anyone. As the dead had no name, no one spoke of the dead, and its presence could not intrude, unwanted, in conversation. Memories were locked away. Jacobo's sense of loss—and everyone's—became as personal as fingerprints.

You can say that Jacobo felt the absence of the horse and missed it, in the sense of missing what it did for him. But if he had deeper feelings for the actual horse, he never let on. He had plenty to think about on his own account. He was seventy-nine years old. With the help of the horse he had enjoyed more mobility and autonomy than any of his contemporaries, even to the point, as Tomás said in his joking way, that he was not just an old man—he was a *caballero*. Now that was in the past. He had a horse no more. He had only what he called his *mulas*—his mules, short for *muletas*, canes.

He no longer patrolled the length of the village to share news and opinions with the other old men, nor could he drag a cedar post or haul barbed wire, as he saw fit, to repair his fences. Every chore grew more difficult. Every project demanded more of him. Merely to check his cattle or irrigate a distant corner of the farm required much walking on weak legs. His labors wore him down, but he never complained, never harkened to how things used to be. Only once did he say in my hearing that he wished he still had the horse, but that was so he could give a grandchild a ride.

After the death of the horse Jacobo kept to himself for a week or so. He remained taciturn, moody. But at last he shook off his depression. He visited, told stories, began anew. His appetite for friendship and work, for teasing and banter, emerged undiminished. He began simply to concentrate his energy in a smaller physical area. And we, fortunate to live and work close by, were among the beneficiaries of the newly tightened focus of his days.

Alex, Anne, and I still lived together in the blue house on the hill. We'd been joined by Susan Norton, who moved in with Alex. Susan was a registered nurse from Louisiana, farm-wise and hard-working, and she quickly developed a fondness for Jacobo and Liza, which they fully reciprocated.

The four of us were Jacobo's closest neighbors, and after the death of

the red horse, he called on us more frequently than ever. Scarcely a day passed that we did not see him, either at the house or in our fields by the canyon mouth. The old man's daily circuit took him to the land across the river that the Americanos still owned and he still managed. If he saw us working, he crossed to visit, returning home by the main village road. We cut back the willows and cleared the stones from the trail that climbed most directly from our fields to the road, and we put a simple bridge where the trail crossed the *acequia* so that he, and we hoped also Liza, would take pleasure in walking to our land.

Being neighbors was a social relationship, but nothing in a small village exists independently of practical considerations. He relied on us and we on him for certain kinds of help, and that interdependence nourished our relationship more richly than affinity alone. Jacobo had lost his horse. He lacked a beast of burden.

And so he said to us:

"Alex, we got to work on that *presa* for the little ditch. You take the axe and this bar. I got the pliers."

"Anna, you are going up the road? Good, I'll get on. I am going too."

"Susanna, Tomás has Copenhagen at the store. Come on, let's get some."

"Bill, maybe tomorrow you bring the truck and we can take these posts to the river."

We carried and drove and hauled, sometimes gladly, sometimes as a matter of routine. Our efforts were always repaid with the currency of the neighborly way: coffee, meals, stories, sympathy, advice, and not least, the loan of tools.

More rooms and buildings on Jacobo's farm were dedicated to storing tools than to sheltering humans or animals. There was an adobe garage, dark and dusty, with all manner of harness hung on the walls. There were two log barns, filled with hay, where forks, hooks, and other tools lay cached in the corners. There was the hollow cottonwood beside the *acequia* that held shovels, bars, and halters. And catty-corner to the main house, with the ditch gurgling in front, there was Lalo's house. Lalo did not live there. His room was in the main house, next to Jacobo's. His house, instead, was devoted to storage.

All three of its downstairs rooms and its copious attic were filled with tools, old tack, and appliances. Some of its walls were painted green and gaily stenciled with hearts and flowers from the days when Jacobo's brother Juan de Jesús and his family lived there. It was a strange retreat, lyrical and utilitarian, smelling of machine oil, kerosene, and apples, which were stored in bins in the farthest room. On one occasion Alex photographed Jacobo and Liza there, Jacobo wearing a yellow hard hat which he'd plucked from the trove of strange and useful implements that crowded every room.

There were hand-forged nippers, hoof knives, and rasps. There were shoeing hammers, claw hammers, and machine hammers. There were post hole diggers, chains, chain clamps, chain hooks, come-alongs, load winches, lariats, picket ropes, picket screws, hobbles, smooth horseshoes and cleated horseshoes. There were cinches, draft collars, singletrees, doubletrees, plowshares, rake tines, baling wire, barbed wire, smooth

wire, wire stretchers, pry bars, tamping bars, digging bars, adzes, draw knives, crosscut and ripping saws, one- and two-man felling saws, pruners, anvils, mauls, picks, brush axes, loppers, pruning shears, tin shears, rivets, sheet leather, strap leather, harness buckles, spare stirrups, baling hooks, bolt cutters, coal shovels, pitchforks, hayrakes, hocks, barrows, and buckets. There were buckets with holes and buckets without, buckets of bolts and buckets of paint. There were saddlebags and washing machines. Mason jars and canners. There were things without names. Things invented. Things broken but useful. Things awaiting repair or a trip to the dump. Things in the corner and things on the floor, usually the very thing you needed, lying unseen beneath and behind the jumble of other things that leaned against the wall.

We borrowed freely.

And every borrowing required a visit, as did the return of the thing borrowed, so that no task existed without a social dimension, without interdependence, without reflection and discussion. We were building fence, grubbing trees, tending horses, butchering cattle. Beginning the spring after the death of the red horse, Anne and I began to build a house. We put away paint brushes and typewriter for masonry and carpentry tools, and we noted with pleasure that Jacobo approved of the newly increased utility of our days.

We chose a site between the top of the hayfield and the ditch. It was occupied by a thicket of wild plums—prunes, Jacobo called them, and he gave the word two syllables, accenting the first: *PRU-ness*. The plums were less attractive than either name suggests. Their fruit blighted every year, and their branches bristled with thorns. If they'd been made of barbed wire instead of wood, they'd have been no less a nuisance and a hazard. We cut them down and pulled the stumps out with the pickup, using chains borrowed from Jacobo. We piled the stiff branches high in the truck and hauled load after load to the bottom of the field.

There were two seeps below the fence where gullies formed, muddy and raw. We ditched above them to keep the irrigation waters from draining through, but the gullies continued to erode because Jacobo's cows trampled or ate any plant that might have taken root to hold the soil. Anne and I resolved to fence out the cattle, using the barbed branches of the plums, a plan Jacobo derided.

It was a struggle to twine the cut plums together. In the process we tore our clothes and earned a score of cuts, but gradually a thorny tangle took shape, worse than a briar patch, encircling the gullies. I figured Jacobo, when he saw it, would finally give in and approve. We'd spent no money; we'd taken a problem—the plums—and turned it into a resource, and built something that looked organic, as though it belonged there. That was Jacobo's way. And the fence was functional. I thought it looked as formidable as the breastworks at Vicksburg.

Toward the end of the second day Jacobo crossed from the Americanos' land to inspect our work. Moments earlier my pride in our accomplishment had diminished somewhat because I'd managed, struggling with the thorns, to cut the tip of my nose, always an embarrassing location for a wound. I was still dabbing the cut with a bandanna when he walked up. Jacobo grinned at the sight of me.

"So," he said, like an officer reviewing troops, "you gonna keep out the cows with that?"

"Yes, it ought to hold."

"No it don't."

"Why not?"

"The cows gonna break it apart."

"But it's tight, they can't break it."

"No, they can. They got tougher noses than you." Jacobo gave a belly laugh, and Anne smiled. I was not amused. Jacobo grabbed a protruding plum branch and yanked. The whole structure rattled and shook.

"I am sorry, Bill, but that fence don't worth a shit. It look like something only a gringo can build."

I felt stung. *Gringo* is a complicated word, especially in the mountains. Depending on inflection, it can be an a term of endearment, a factual descriptor, or a gauntlet flung down. Coming from Jacobo it seemed an epitaph: *here lies Bill deBuys, gringo. He always had more ideas than sense.*

I was so furious I could not speak.

"Why don't you use posts and wire?" he continued.

"We had to do something with these prunes, so we put 'em to good use," I answered.

"Just throw 'em away in the arroyo. Same thing for any weed."

"I like 'em here. Anyway, this fence will hold."

"Hmmm. We gonna see." Jacobo helped himself to a pinch of Copenhagen. He spat. "We gonna see," he said again, and his tone was that of a teacher who recognizes that certain students are beyond help and that instruction must finally yield to fate.

"Bill, Anne," he said, "I got to go move my water," and leaning heavily on his canes he descended to the ford where he waded the river again.

Next morning I went early to the gringo fence, which now could have no other name. Nose scabbed and ego raw, I wrestled again with the thorns, reaching deep in the bramble to tie together the plum branches with baling wire. At the cost of more cuts and potential ridicule, I reinforced every yard of it and added bulwarks of cottonwood logs to give it mass. The wire was invisible from outside the fence.

Weeks passed and the vegetation protected by the gringo fence grew sweet. The cows probed and tested. The fence held. Jacobo inspected it several times, poking with his canes or grabbing where it was free of thorns and shaking hard.

On one occasion I happened by while he was testing it.

"Jacobo, how do you like that fence now? Not bad for a gringo, eh?"

"You don't say you gonna tie it together with wire."

"Wire?"

"Sure," he gave it a hefty yank. "Got to be wire to hold it like that."

"Well, sure—wire," I said. "Of course I used wire. That's the only way to make it strong enough."

Jacobo frowned. "Is that so? Well, maybe it can hold. Anyway, for a while." He shook his head.

We stood there a while in silence, Jacobo gazing toward the river. He had a dose of snuff in his mouth and slowly churned it, ruminating, so that he looked only slightly more philosophical than his cows. I poked and bothered the fence a bit, testing it the way he had done. I saw that a few canes of raspberry I'd planted in the seep were sprouting leaves, but I realized it wouldn't do, for the moment, to point that out to Jacobo.

Finally, Jacobo stretched himself to his full height and pointed a cane across the river. He said, "Anyway, seems to me that yellow cow dropped her calf in those oaks. I got to find it."

"I'll help you."

"*Bueno*, come on," he said, already marching toward the river. I scrambled to keep up.

There was a time when the word *gringo* held little friendly meaning for Jacobo. He'd worked with Anglos occasionally "at the sheeps," but over the years most of his partners were Hispano. The few gringos he'd been thrown with had been "all right," he said, by which you further understood he'd barely tolerated them. And there was the young *tejano* at the CCC camps during the Depression, whom he would have flayed with a with a butcher knife if the *sanavabitch* hadn't run so fast.

What turned him around on gringos was his daughters—and his gringo sons-in-law. The addition of non-Hispanos to the family, moreover, was the result of Jacobo's own striving.

He had two great goals in life. One was to buy out his brothers and sisters and own his father's farm. The other was to educate his children. Lalo, however, never had a chance at education. Like his father, he went to work as a herder as soon as he was old enough, and from that point on, his earnings were important to the well-being of the entire family.

Macario was next in line. In about 1939, Jacobo and Liza enrolled him in the eighth grade at the Allison James School in Santa Fe, which, like Menaul, was a Presbyterian boarding school. Jacobo and Liza were then Catholics, but the available Catholic schools, they had discovered, were too expensive, and the local public schools were simply not good enough—their students learned little English, and English was the key to a practical education. At Allison James, the Romeros were obliged to pay only fifty percent of Macario's tuition. The boy was given a job to earn the balance.

Macario completed one year, but early in the second, he fought with the principal and left. That was the end of formal education for him, and his younger brothers, Eliu and Jake, eventually showed no greater patience for schooling. They were difficult, like their father. "Each boy was twice as hard as any girl," Liza says. "If I had more boys instead of girls, I don't know if I could make it."

The girls, however, cared for school, and Liza and Jacobo encouraged their interest. Luisa, the oldest, remembers her father saying that he did not want his daughters growing up to marry in the mountains and "have only a pickup full of kids." He wanted more for them than that. Luisa was sent to Allison James after Macario left, and she did well. One of the first things the teachers taught her—a sign of the times in those days before cultural diversity was counted a good thing—was to spell her name the English way, *Louisa*, and so it has remained.

The next year Louisa went to Menaul, eventually graduating in 1946. Edna came close behind her, and Fabiola, known to everyone as Faby, followed Edna. These were hard years for the Romero family. Lalo joined the Army in 1942, and except for his earnings as a G.I., they might not have scraped together the tuitions. Times were hard in other ways, too. Lalo was sent to the Pacific. He was a medic, in combat. Some nights, Liza worried so much for him that she could not sleep. Rising from bed, she would go to the porch and stare at a big star, wishing she could be on that star so that she could look down on Lalo and see if he was safe. She spent three years like that, fearing the bad news that, fortunately, never came.

One day the Catholic priest in Peñasco summoned Jacobo and Liza to a meeting. It wasn't about Lalo. And it wasn't about the upcoming *función* at the El Valle church—*la fiesta de San Miguel*—for which Jacobo and Liza had dutifully agreed to serve as *mayordomos* and provide the food. The priest was concerned about another matter.

"You must not send your daughters to Presbyterian schools," he lectured them. "That is wrong. We have good Catholic schools you can send them to."

"But the Catholic schools cost too much," Jacobo protested.

"That is not the important thing," the priest said. He would not relent. He gave them an ultimatum, "Take your children out of the Presbyterian schools, or else you will have to leave the Church."

"All right, then." Jacobo did not hesitate. "We will leave." He stood up. He regularly gave money to the Church, along with his labor and time, but he was not a true believer. He had not tasted communion, for instance, since his wedding mass, in 1921.

The priest warned him of the consequences to his soul.

"We are leaving," Jacobo repeated. And forthwith Jacobo and Liza, who was as ready as he to change churches, worshipped with the Presbyterians. Accordingly, the *función* took place without them, and the children stayed in school.

As Jacobo had hoped, education improved his daughters' prospects in life. Edna met a student from the University of New Mexico, George Maestas, who boarded at Menaul. When George graduated, in 1949, they married. It was time of great pride for the entire Romero family, for not only did Edna marry an educated man with a bright future, but the ceremony was performed by Edna's cousin Porfirio, the son of Amador, who had recently been ordained a Presbyterian minister. This was how things were supposed to go.

Then Faby broke the mold. She was graduated from Menaul in 1950 and stayed on in Albuquerque to attend business and secretarial school. The city thronged with soldiers and airmen based at Sandia and Kirtland. In the fall of '50 Faby met a flight mechanic from Kirtland named Jim Skaggs. They dated for a few months, and then Jim received orders for temporary duty in Chicago. Faby didn't follow, but the letters flew back and forth between them. Their certainty about each other grew, and they made plans to marry as soon as Jim returned to Albuquerque in April.

Jacobo was in Wyoming when he learned the news. Faby recalls that "he wasn't too thrilled." Jacobo wrote to Liza and Lalo urging them to persuade Faby not to go through with the wedding. "Faby doesn't know what she's getting into," he argued. "Gringos don't like Mexican people."

But Liza and Lalo didn't try to stop her. Lalo, the ex-G.I., who now had more experience than his father in the gringo world, told his mother, "If this is what Faby wants, let her do it. If she says this Jim Skaggs is a good man, probably he is."

Lalo had just bought a new Ford. In it, in fine style, he, Liza, and Macario drove to sister Faby's wedding. At that time Liza spoke little English and did not understand much of what Jim Skaggs said to her, but she watched her prospective son-in-law closely as the festivities progressed. By the time the ceremony was over, she had determined that the young man was all right.

She wrote and told Jacobo so, but still he smoldered. He did not scold Faby, but it was plain in his letters to her that he did not approve. Faby wrote back, "It's your fault, Daddy. You sent us to school in the city." To make matters worse, when Jacobo returned to El Valle, some of the other men in the village criticized him for letting his daughter marry a gringo. The social consequences of Faby's act were not easy to bear.

Faby and Jim soon came for a visit. Jim remembers, "Jacobo didn't know what to do, whether to shake my hand or hug me—so he hugged me." Still, acceptance was not automatic. It took time for Jim's good nature to win Jacobo over. On regular visits to the homeplace Jim was invariably easygoing, good-humored, imperturbable. And he treated Fabby well. In spite of himself, Jacobo grew to like him.

On reflection, he might not have been too surprised by Faby's choice. His own sister Sophía had been the first of the Romero clan to marry outside *la gente*, as well as one of the first to enjoy an education. When brother Avelino died in World War I, his military life insurance helped pay her tuition at Allison James. The English she learned enabled her eventually to take a job as a nanny with an Anglo family in Santa Fe. When the family moved to Iowa, she moved with them and there met and married Arch Ledbetter, a gringo.

Now Faby had crosed the line, and soon, so did Louisa, who had taken a job in the finance center at Holloman Air Base in Alamogordo. There she met Norman Rogers. When Norm was transferred to a base in Tennessee, Louisa agreed to go with him, as his bride. The wedding was held in Norm's hometown of Lansing, Michigan in March of 1952. Neither Jacobo nor Liza attended, and Jacobo, once again, did not approve. Louisa told him, "Dad, you have to accept it," but still acceptance took time.

The passage of time made things easier, but not necessarily smooth, for other Anglos, also servicemen, who courted other daughters. Billy married Ruth, Melvin married Evila, Michael married Eva, and Russ married Frances. In fact, it was not Jacobo's way to welcome any suitor of his daughters with open arms, not even Clarence Mascareñas from nearby Vadito. Clarence eventually married Naomi and became Jacobo's only Hispano son-in-law besides George Maestas. Clarence remembers one day seeking out Jacobo to ask permission to take Naomi on an errand to Peñasco. Jacobo was in a field irrigating. He scarcely looked up while Clarence stated his request. The young man waited politely while Jacobo thought it over. Then Jacobo raised his head. There was fury in his eyes. "*¡Pintate pa'l infierno!*" he snapped. "Go to hell!" For years afterward Clarence bragged he knew where Hell was—it was Peñasco because that was where he went when he was told to go there. And in spite of Jacobo, he took Naomi along.

Except for Lalo, all the children married. Eliu wedded a girl from Taos Pueblo, which was another shock to Jacobo. Jake married a *hispana* from Taos town. The family grew. But it mainly grew in distant states and cities. Only Macario, who returned to the mountains after a long stint at the mines in Grants, settled down to raise a family close to home. Before long, Jacobo and Liza had several dozen grandchildren, a majority of whom spoke no Spanish and belonged almost wholly to the world beyond the mountains. It was unfortunate, Jacobo said, not being able to speak Spanish with so many of his *nietos*. It meant he couldn't teach them as much, couldn't give them all he had to give. But those English-speaking children were family, and family was family. Anyway, he'd say, most kids these days won't listen to you—in any language.

By the time Alex, Anne, and I arrived in the village, Jacobo had long been accustomed to gringos. Still, we appeared more disreputable than most, certainly than his clean-cut sons-in-law. Our hair was long, our work habits strange, and we lived with little visible means of support. Each of us at various times taught school for short periods. Sometimes I worked as a carpenter in Española or Taos. And, strange to tell, I'd received a reward for finding the airplane and the *difuntos* in the mountains. By various means, we got by.

We were an odd lot, obviously. But we were also neighbors, which in Jacobo's view seemed to entitle us to the benefit of the doubt on matters relating to character.

Building a house reflected well on character. Perhaps we—and in particular, I—had deficiencies where fencing, gopher gassing, and the inutility of working at a typewriter were concerned, but the building of a house at least showed industry. In Jacobo's scale of values stupidity could be excused. Sloth could not.

Anne and I quarried adobes for our house from a building in Truchas, nearly a century old, that had been gutted by fire. The bricks were thick and strong, weighing more than thirty pounds apiece. Even when we dropped them from the tops of the charred walls, they did not break. We chipped them clean of the old mud mortar, and on some we found footprints of goats and barefoot children.

Jacobo helped us unload adobes from the truck. Face furrowed, he studied the footprints with mock seriousness.

"I know that one!" he said. "That is my uncle's foot. What a mean man."

"Which one, Jacobo? The footprint with toes or the one from a hoof?"

"This one's got toes, but he must have had a hoof somewhere to be so mean."

Every place and time has its work banter. Hard-hats outcuss each other, and allusions are mostly sexual: "Will you hurry up with that bolt?" The answer comes back: "Can't find the hole. Got no hair around it!"

With Jacobo the materials and tools became animate: "This brick *no quiere*. It don't want to fit." Or, "Maybe you hit your thumb because that hammer's mad at you, or maybe you mad at yourself."

When it came time to pour the footing, he helped us collect a ton or more of river cobbles from the Americanos' field. The scattered rocks interfered with irrigation, and they were useful to us because by throwing them in the footing we saved on cement. Jacobo limped from truck to stone and back to truck as we filled the bed of the pickup. It was heavy work. By the time we drove the load back to the house site, my back ached, and I was ready to slow down. Not Jacobo. "Come on," he said, "Let's get these sons-a-bitchy rocks out of the truck. We're not through working yet."

Near the house site Anne found a chunk of limestone with fossils in it. Such rocks were fairly common in outcrops along the ditch.

"Look here, Jacobo," she said, "There are clams in the rocks."

Jacobo studied it carefully. "I live all my life here," he said with some amazement, "and I never notice anything like this. These things are fish, no? How do they get here?"

"Scientists say this land was under an ocean once."

He looked Anne hard in the eye, then me, to be sure we weren't putting him on. Then for a moment he reflected.

"Yes, they could have an ocean here, I guess. In the time of *Noé*, they say, water covered even the mountains."

"In the time of who?"

"*Noé*. Who built the ark."

"Some flood, eh?"

"Some flood."

Day by day the walls of the house slowly rose, and Jacobo frequently stopped by to sit in the shade of a tall juniper and chat with Anne as she mixed the mud we used as mortar. We brought water to the site by siphoning it from the irrigation ditch through a garden hose. When Jacobo saw water flowing from the hose, he scolded us for putting a "pipe" in the ditch. "They don't let you do that," he said. "The ditch can break from that." We showed him that the hose went over, not through, the ditchbank. "Where is the pump?" he asked. We said, look, there is the hose; you can see there is no pump. He said, "Then how do you make the water jump the ditch?" We tried to explain the siphon, but in vain. "You know too much," he said, and shook his head.

Apart from the siphon Jacobo generally approved of the way we built our house, relying on ourselves for labor and scrounging materials. The adobes were secondhand, the mud and stones free. Lumber for forms and scaffolding was salvaged from other buildings and jobs. For lintels and door frames we bought six by sixteens and two by sixteens from a local sawmill. It was beautiful wood, old-growth ponderosa from the Jemez Mountains. We planed the timbers by hand, and left them exposed in the walls of the finished house, with no additional casings or jambs.

With the walls up we needed roof beams, *vigas*, which are whole trees, peeled of bark. We paid the Forest Service $8.32 for the right to cut down thirteen trees. Even on our budget, it was a deal. That was the easy part. To get the trees we had to go halfway to Taos, to the far side of a mountain called U.S. Hill, then fourteen miles on a rough, steep logging road to the top of a mountain divide that separated the waters of the Rio Grande from those of the Mississippi. There we could have our pick of standing dead spruce trees, if we thought we could get them home. We teamed with Jacobo's nephew, Gerson Romero, the son of Juan de Dios, who needed a similar load, and formed a crew of about fifteen, with Jacobo as self-appointed foreman. It was the kind of expedition the old man loved. Much labor was needed, and laborers needed instruction.

A week earlier Anne and I had scouted the mountain and found a promising stand of trees. We led the caravan of trucks and trailers there, carefully turned the vehicles around on the narrow truck trail, and fanned out to begin selecting and cutting trees. The slope was steep and the forest was choked with wind-felled timber, so progress was slow.

Too slow for Jacobo. He stalked through the trees on his canes, giving orders with every breath: "Cut this one. No! That one is too crooked. Come over here."

"That's too far from the truck, Jacobo. Come back this way. We don't want to drag it so far."

"No, you can drag 'em. It's not far. Come on. Good. You too, come over. You better cut this one. No, this one right here. Now, start that saw. Pull on the starter. Pull again. Pull again. *Jalalo.* We got a problem. *Este no quiere.* Bring that other saw. This one is no good. Now start 'em. *Jalalo. Dale* gas. Okay, now cut. Make the notch. You need to drop him over there. Cut the wedge. Right there. Go ahead. *Andale.* Cut him now. Good. Make the other cut. Come over here. Start a little lower. Now cut 'em there, straight through. All the way. He gonna go. Get back. *¡Cuidado!* There he goes! He gonna hit that tree! Now he hit him. Now he's caught. He don't fall any more. Oh, you cut him wrong. Now we got another problem."

The newly cut tree leans against another. The sun angles against it,

through a geometry of gray trunks. Mixed among the chain saw exhaust and wood smells is the aroma of whortleberry crushed beneath our boots. We sit on logs or sprawl on the duff, passing the water bottle. The old man wears a broad-brimmed, five-and-dime straw hat with a white cord fastened under his chin. He takes a pinch of snuff, puts the tin back in the shirt pocket, which like all his shirt pockets is frayed at the bottom around the arc of the tin. He works his toothless jaws. In a minute he spits, and starts again: "Come on, bring those ropes. We gonna pull him down. Where is the saw? Get the saw, come on." And he staggers off on his canes, as though chasing them. "Come on. Come on. These *vigas* don't get on the trailer by theirself!"

The *vigas* we hauled were twenty-six feet long. We pulled the last load down the mountain as darkness fell. The truck's radiator had begun to leak, and we'd hitched up the flimsy trailer that carried the *vigas* without a safety chain, but I didn't care. I was elated. We had the *vigas* and we were headed home. When we got to the pavement at the bottom of U.S. Hill, I drove fast.

Anne was in the cab with me, and Alex and another friend were in the back. Once we topped the hill, we picked up speed. I could feel the truck sway side to side as we raced down the mountain. Alex banged on the back window and shouted something. He seemed elated, too. As a matter of fact, he banged and shouted many times on the drive back to El Valle. He must have been extremely elated.

But his mood was different when I parked the truck at home. "You idiot-fool-*pendejo*!" he shouted, leaping down from the truck bed. "You could have got us killed."

"What do you mean?"

"The trailer nearly jack-knifed a hundred times out there. Why didn't you slow down when I told you to?" Alex was spouting more steam than the radiator of the truck. It was unnerving to see him so worked up.

"Guess I couldn't hear you. Sorry." I realized I was seriously at fault. It was not an unfamiliar feeling. "Here," I said, "have a beer."

He took it, but it took more than one to cool him.

We peeled the *vigas* with draw knives borrowed from Jacobo and fastened them to the wooden bond beam with giant lag bolts. Since the house was only sixteen feet deep, the *vigas* spanned it with plenty to spare. We left the small ends of the beams cantilevering past the front wall to support a roof for the porch. Then we nailed boards of rough-sawn, one-inch spruce to the tops of the *vigas*, making both a ceiling and a deck for roofing material.

With each visit Jacobo studied the jutting beams above the porch with greater puzzlement. He didn't like what he saw. "When you gonna put the posts for the porch?" he asked.

We told him we didn't need posts and described how the cantilever worked. Our efforts to explain were as unsuccessful as they had been with the siphon. He said we better think about it and put some posts. A day or two later he returned and asked whether we had the porch posts ready. We told him we wouldn't be using any, that the *vigas* were strong and well anchored and there was no need for additional support.

He seemed irritated. "You know too much," he said again, by which he left small doubt he thought we knew too little.

Woodpile Canto

Feliz cumpleaños *this June morning. You pick a good day to be eighty, or any age. Around us the valley warms to the sun. I hear a blackbird on a fencepost, a towhee in the orchard. And here by the woodpile, magpies squawk.*

You remember, years ago, when Lalo brought this wood? He dragged it with the team from a canyon too steep for any truck, and over the ridge behind us.

You don't see piñon like this anymore. The smallest stump is older than the village. On the largest you can count back rings to the thin, dry year when Oñate crossed the deserts up from Mexico.

It was November when Lalo cut the trees and limbed them. Next day, he brought the horses, which you had shod. Four shoes on the ancient red but only front ones for the roan. He was too mean, and his bone-hard hooves defied the nippers, so you trimmed them with an axe.

Lalo and the team made five trips. Each time he looped a chain thick as your arm around the trunks and hooked it to the singletree.

Then he whistled. The red horse leaned into the collar and the roan lunged, hooves digging deep, chains snapping taut, logs slamming and twisting. The load cut its way forward like a blunt-nosed plow, furrowing the grove, departing after centuries.

Climbing from the canyon, Lalo rested the horses where the trail flattened, and again at the top. Their sides heaved and their breath watered the air. On the other side descending, he balanced on the load, whistling shrill enough to stir the owls and singing "Arbol de esperanza," *as the logs ground together like millstones and left a trail of bark.*

It took two days to buck the logs to length, but now the pile is made: straight-splitting, long-burning, clear piñon. Wood so old will have some rot, but you can smell the pitch. It has the smell of warmth and winter both.

This is good wood, and the land would grow it again in time, if we let it. But we don't. This is the day of the chain saw and the four-wheel drive. The day of the old wood is past; soon the little that remains will find its way to hearths and stoves like yours.

We can grieve for these hard-used hills, for the soil that washed away and the grass that doesn't grow. For the great gray stumps that rot in silence. And we can elegize the lives that hauled the wood and felt its warmth, lives that are ended, or ending.

But wait.

For now, let's applaud the passing years, the good and the bad. Feliz cumplea- ños, *old man. It is a good day to be eighty, or any age.*

The air is cool as the land warms toward noon. The blackbirds, towhees, and magpies sing in chorus. We pause, as you pause by the wood, thinking on eighty years in harness. You rest a while, then go to fetch your splitting maul and wedge.

11

Retratos

Anne and I saw less of Jacobo as the house consumed more of our efforts and the finish work grew more exacting. Alex, meanwhile, saw more of him. The nature of his partnership with Jacobo was different from ours. Alex was building no house. He was less preoccupied with fences and farmwork than we. Instead he carried a camera, which he focused more and more on the old man.

He might have been drawn differently to Jacobo, had it not been for his work in Alaska. Alex's far northern experiences, particularly in the remote Eskimo villages of the southern Bering Sea coast, broadened his approach to photography. He found it at first unsettling and then energizing that the snapshots pinned to the walls in the homes of his Eskimo hosts displayed a sense of playfulness and spontaneity that was absent from the severe, wistful, and brooding portraits he was making. He began to loosen up, to expand the range of the moods and situations that he considered photographically appropriate, and to make a greater effort to see his subjects, amidst all the ordinariness of their daily lives, in the light they saw themselves.

He was charmed by one old Eskimo man whose family he accompanied to a summer fishing camp called Chilugan. There, gathered in the family's big tent during hours of rest in the long near-arctic days, the old man held court, teasing his grandchildren, telling jokes, telling stories that were like short, one-man plays. He acted them out with animal voices, elaborate gestures, and a quality of facial and physical expressiveness that conveyed as much of the story as the words themselves. It was storytelling such as Homer must have done, and although the old man spoke only

Inuit, Alex felt he understood the stories well. The photographs that resulted are among the strongest of an extraordinary collection, which is admired no less by critics than by the subjects themselves.

Returning home to El Valle, Alex began to notice in Jacobo some of the qualities he had admired in the old Eskimo. There was the same centered gentleness, the same motility of face and hands, the same wholeness of the storyteller's art. He soon faced an ironic realization: just as I had discovered late in my attempt to write history that my most important source was a garrulous next door neighbor, Alex came back from the top of the hemisphere to learn that the essence of what he'd been drawn to document in Alaska also existed, even flourished, a few minutes' walk down the road.

It was a liberating idea, which he soon had the resources to pursue thanks both to a Guggenheim fellowship and to the fact that for the first time in six years he was not working in specific collaboration with Robert Coles. He was on his own. He bought a four-by-five view camera and began experimenting with it, shooting color as well as black and white. In particular he shot landscapes and house interiors in the mountain villages. He also began accompanying Jacobo and helping with his daily chores. Always a camera—either a 2¼-inch Hasselblad, which he'd used extensively in Alaska, or an even more portable 35mm Nikon—was with him. When the work slowed or the moment seemed right, he raised it to his eye and pressed the shutter.

Other members of the Romero family marveled that Alex took so many pictures of Jacobo. Liza would nod and say, "Alex spends too much time with Jacobo." She didn't mean necessarily that the action was excessive, as when one says, "You talk too much." She meant simply that the time Alex spent with her *viejo* was an amount so great that it surpassed rational understanding. Alex's behavior was quirky, *loco*, *estrambótico*. But then, so were a lot of things.

People sometimes think that small communities are engines of conformity, but nothing could be further from the truth. In our village nearly everyone was blatantly eccentric in one way or another. Jacobo irrigated in the rain. Another man, half-blind, drove his pickup truck as though by Braille, and people pulled off the road when they saw him coming. Alex's peculiarity was that he took "too many" pictures and bore a camera seemingly attached to his anatomy, like a large goiter. It was a bad habit, but not a dangerous one, and people forgave him for it.

While no one else understood why Alex wanted to take so many pictures of Jacobo, the old man never questioned it. The relationship between the two of them was a partnership. On one level it was a simple trade. Jacobo needed Alex's help. He could not drive a truck. Sometimes he could not carry all the tools he needed where he needed them. And stretching wire or herding cattle, two men were always better than one. So as neighbors exchanging labor, Alex gave Jacobo a hand, and Jacobo gave Alex opportunities to make pictures.

On another level, Jacobo welcomed the attention. Sometimes he visited in the darkroom while Alex printed pictures from their hours together. He liked to stare into the developer bath and watch his likeness form under the red light. "Oh, what a handsome man," he'd say. "Where do you find such a handsome man around here?" And he would study his image with a kind of detachment, as though it surprised him the image was his own.

Jacobo was no egotist, but he could see that the photographs spoke strongly of him, of his work and his place. He took satisfaction in participating in that statement, and maybe, in his private thoughts, he saw it as a legacy. When a print went into the waste can, as many inevitably did, he'd bid it a mournful, self-mocking good-bye: "There goes poor Jacobo. Maybe we don't see that old man again. Pretty nice man, they say, but he's gone now."

More important than matters of vanity or mutual aid, the two *liked* each other. Just as no social relationship in a village can exist entirely outside of practical considerations, no work relationship can exist without also being a social one. Alex felt that the photographs were not so much the reason for spending the day with Jacobo as the justification for it. He wanted to help, wanted Jacobo to think he was a good worker—a good man—as they irrigated, worked cows, brought in the hay. But the forward-directed, work-oriented voice in the back of his head insisted, "You can't do that, can't fritter away your days doing someone else's farmwork. You are a photographer. You *must* take pictures." And so in the midst of chores of various kinds he wore the camera, and used it. That quieted the voice.

There was no thought then that the resulting photographs might find their way into a book. Alex simply made them, developed the negatives, printed contact sheets and filed the lot away, scarcely knowing what he had. And then went out the next day to do it again, ambling down to the Romero house shortly after breakfast to inquire what the day's work would be.

Alex made a point of being available for the major jobs, haying in particular. A sense of deliverance came with the hard work of putting up the hay. By late summer irrigation had become arduous drudgery, made worse by the tall grass that choked the *regaderas* and obscured the patterns of the water, blinding the irrigator to the effect of his labor. The fields became alien. You did not wade into the waist-high grass for fear of trampling future harvest. You stood at the edges, looking in, a spectator to the life of the field, watching breezes ripple the seed heads. You took inconvenient detours along the pasture margins, for the more direct routes were closed to you. When finally the hay was cut, then raked, baled, and hauled away, the field was like a possession returned. Its space became available again, and the expansion of your freedom to move in that space harmonized with the other, more tangible rewards of harvest.

Putting up the hay from a big field like Jacobo's requires recruitment of

grandchildren and friends. Someone gasses the truck; maybe an extra truck is borrowed. You keep an anxious eye on the afternoon clouds that swell above the peaks, and you gather work boots, gloves, and, in spite of the August heat, a long-sleeved shirt sturdy enough to protect your arms from the abrasion of the bales. Alex, meanwhile, also loads a roll of Tri-X into the heavy-bodied Nikon, which he slings over his shoulder.

Everyone takes pride in working fast. Ideally each truck has a crew of four: one to drive, one in the back of the truck to stack the load, and two on either side to lift the bales and throw them in the pickup. The bales weigh close to seventy pounds, more if the hay is still a little wet, and you always feel competitive, at least at the outset, to show you can heave a bale to the top of a high load, to show you can keep up and even stay ahead of the rest of the crew, as you warm to the work, cut a sweat, and with each heave send a shower of grass seeds and hay dust down your collar.

Jacobo's age prevented him from working with a regular crew so he generally trudged ahead of the truck using a longshoreman's hook, or

gancho, to gather scattered bales into groups of two and three so that they might be loaded faster. He regularly paused and critically surveyed the loading operation, quick to point out if the bales were liable to spill. There was a pictorial quality to the tableau: the top-heavy truck, the tracks from the baling equipment striping the field in parallel curves, the bales at even intervals like headstones, and finally the old man, grim-faced, chest heaving, toiling toward the truck, hay bale in tow. Alex seizes the moment to step back, swab the sweat from his eyes as he removes the lens cap, and quickly: click. Then on to another bale.

About thirty-four bales make a full load and then the workers crowd into the cab or cling to perches atop the bales, and the truck, roaring in low gear and swaying side to side, inches loudly up the slope toward the barn.

There the crew redeploys: one or two throw bales from the truck onto the dirt roof of what was once a sheep pen; a relay thrower then hurls them into the shaded, dusty interior of the barn. Alex takes the job of stacker, inside the barn, stowing the bales in tight ranks where they will remain through most of the coming winter, or perhaps several winters.

His Nikon hangs from his shoulder like a clumsy bandoleer. He pushes it behind him, out of the way, but with the leaning, lifting, pivoting, and heaving of bales, it keeps slipping to the front. There is no place to put it down—every surface in the barn is temporary, soon vanishing as the space fills with hay. The dangling camera interferes with his work. His job is hardest. The relay thrower on the roof of the sheep pen, one of Macario's sons, only has to toss the bales into the barn, but Alex, working against gravity, must not only lift them, but stack them tightly in well-ordered positions. It will not do to place them sloppily. At least three and maybe four more loads must be brought up from the field, and there must be room in the barn for all of them. Jacobo leans into the barn through a low, crude door and watches Alex to be sure he is stacking them right.

Try as he may, Alex falls behind. The bales pile up on the floor of the barn as the second thrower heaves them in. Alex works faster, anxious to avoid Jacobo's displeasure. Even so, he notices that the second thrower is silhouetted against distant mountains and that the barn is slowly filling with hay dust, which catches the sunlight filtering through the slats of the roof and makes the interior faintly luminous. The old man leaning

through the doorway adds an incongruous element. Alex senses that a photograph of what he sees will make sense only if he catches a bale in flight; otherwise no one will understand the action that unites the figures in the scene.

Quickly he throws down his gloves, removes the lens cap, and shoots twice as the relay thrower hurls two bales. Then fast as he can, replaces the lens cap, trying hard not to drip sweat on the lens, slings the camera behind his back and jumps down to heave the bales in place. Then he shoots again, retrieves the bales and steals another shot. He falls behind. Shoots again. And falls behind still further. He takes twelve shots in all; in ten of them a bale is in midair, in two he shot too late. Maybe he got something good. More likely he didn't. He works feverishly to catch up, in spite of the fact that a little delay will hurt no one, least of all Jacobo, who is not paying him for his labor, but he cannot bear Jacobo's thinking he's less than *un buen trabajador*.

Taking pictures has slowed things, and Alex has not caught up. Still, he cannot let the chance pass. Again he throws down his gloves and raises the camera. Jacobo leans farther in the door, and Alex can feel him counting the bales that lie jumbled on the floor. Jacobo scowls. The relay thrower throws. The shutter clicks. Thirteenth.

Again, on with the lens cap and gloves, and down into the jumble to heave the bales in place. Much later, in the darkroom, Alex sees that it's the thirteenth shot that is the good one. It has the bale in the air, the distant mountains, the light slanting through. But what makes it work is the gnomish posture of the old man leaning through the partly blocked doorway, the old man whose scowl gives the picture its pith, and whose evident displeasure was the one thing Alex did not want to see.

Photographers are made by their subjects, and the best subjects have the quality of being self-possessed without being self-conscious. They know how to "be themselves."

The photographer says, "just be yourself." And you think, "Easy for you to say." But you don't say it because the lens is pointed at you. Your mind begins to race: is your hair in your face? Your fly zipped? Is your mouth in the same pout that has plagued you in every photograph all your life? It's either the pout or the smirk. Quick, decide!

Jacobo never had to decide. He had a gift few people share. He had the ability to project aspects of himself, to wear naturally the smile or squint that fit the situation. The quality he had went beyond being photogenic. It was an instinct for self-projection, a presence, a centeredness. It was much the same quality that attracted us to him as a person. And it allowed him to look into a camera without defensiveness.

I read somewhere that singers do well in the movies because they've learned the trick of projecting themselves naturally, even when—especially when—the attention of an audience is on them. To be a storyteller in a village is not far different from being a singer, and Jacobo, like the old Eskimo in Chilugan, was accustomed to holding the attention of others. He expected and welcomed it. The camera may have been a newcomer to his audience, but there was a place for it. In the hands of a friend and neighbor, it was welcome.

Photography thrives on accident. The careworn brow of the woman, staring into the distance, baby at her breast, may derive from heartache or heartburn, we don't know which, but the picture stolen in that moment by the photographer is nonetheless poignant. It stands for more, perhaps, than what it literally represents. In photographing Jacobo, however, Alex faced the opposite problem. Knowing Jacobo as friend and neighbor, not as photographic subject, he felt his photographs were always playing catch-up to what he wanted to capture. The understandings the photographs embodied weren't false, but they were partial. More could always have been said; a truer, more complete image might always be caught.

It was not enough to show Jacobo as he moved through his world. Alex also wanted to show him as he, Alex, felt he knew him, and the act of photography was the means for exploring those feelings. It was essential, if the work were to be true to either of them, that the photographs provoke a sense of recognition, that Jacobo be able to say, "yes, that is me; I am there." But it was no less essential that the photographs carry a sense of revelation, a sense of complexity captured, a fullness of time, place, man, and relationship.

Alex took basically two kinds of photographs of Jacobo. With his 35mm camera he made candid pictures of Jacobo at work or telling stories. With the beat-up Hasselblad and his brand-new view camera, he made portraits. The large-format portraits were, by necessity, premeditated. Using a big camera on a tripod, Alex chose a view, selected a context, created a situation. But the contexts he chose consisted of Jacobo's buildings, tools, and possessions, things the old man had used or tended for years, in a sense burnishing them with his identity.

A portrait is at its best when it embodies a sense of *time*, when it seems to say that much experience and many individual moments have been distilled into the instant of the photograph. Alex's portraits of Jacobo touch that quality. Each reflects a different aspect of the old man's character, but all possess a common mood of patience. They seem to say, "we have been waiting a long time for the elements of what you see here to converge, for this moment to come. Now it has. It has come to this, which is true."

The making of a portrait started with affection for a particular place. Alex, for instance, walked by Jacobo's main barn, sometimes several times a day. The barn faced the village road and looked so broken-down and out of square that it possessed a kind of arrogance. No other building in the village so blatantly defied gravity. In the sixty or seventy years since its construction, the barn's main posts had shifted and the entire roof traveled south a good yard or more. Its resistance to collapse appeared less structural than metaphysical.

Alex knew the barn well and frequently contemplated it as he walked by. More than once he helped fill it with hay or, in the corral beside it, helped wrestle Jacobo's cattle through the castrations, ear-slittings, de-hornings, and other useful tortures that punctuated ranch life. In spite of the harshness of the work it sheltered, the place itself, because it was so lived in, was welcoming and familiar.

Usually Alex took pictures in early morning or late afternoon, when angled light and strong shadows emphasized the definition of things. The inside of Jacobo's barn, however, took on an unusual quality at midday.

When the sun was high, the inside of the barn seemed a sanctuary, cool and sweet smelling. Hay bales, stacked to the rafters, walled in the quiet space, creating an architecture both grand and geometric. On the grid of hay bales lay a second grid. Bars of sunlight streamed through cracks between the roof boards and boldly striped the interior. Alex was attracted to the vault of space, dark and cool, with angled light. He decided he would try to photograph Jacobo there.

On a day when the old man was not irrigating, he carried his four-by-five view camera and its bulky tripod and accessories down the road and called at the Romero house shortly before noon. He stowed his gear in the shade of the porch, where the film would stay cool. The old man came to the door and told him to come in.

Jacobo and Liza were sitting down to lunch. The pressure cooker, cooling, hissed weakly on the stove. Bowls of potatoes, beans, and meat, cooked as always to extreme softness to accommodate toothless gums, crowded the table beside dishes of chile, stacks of white bread and cups of coffee. In the center of the table stood a wooden cup, useless to Jacobo, which was filled with toothpicks and bore a little sign on the side that read, "Here's a toothpick, nice and clean, to pick around and in between."

Alex sat down and Liza gave him a plate. In Alex's case the customary invitation to eat was understood and therefore omitted. Her absolute hospitality required that he not leave until he had helped himself to generous portions of all that was offered. He did not protest.

For twenty or thirty minutes they ate and chatted, sharing observations about weather, neighbors, and notorious animals.

Finally, as Jacobo handed an empty plate to Liza and pushed back his chair, Alex said, "I was looking in the barn. It's beautiful in there now. I wonder do you know where I can find a good-looking old man to sit in there to take a picture?"

Jacobo stroked his chin solemnly. "Could be pretty hard. We don't have too many 'round here," he said. "But maybe I can find one."

Then Liza snorted, "Well maybe you can find him in a clean shirt old man, because you are too *cochino* to have your picture taken. Look at you!" And she was right. The pocket of Jacobo's shirt was torn, and the breast was stained red with chile.

Jacobo looked down and with big stiff fingers brushed away what he could of the chile. Abashed, he smiled, "Well, I can put another shirt."

Alex felt a wave of worry. True, the shirt the old man was wearing was a mess, but it suited Jacobo; it was worn and hard-used, entirely fitting the old man's character. Alex feared Jacobo might change to something too formal. He watched him hobble down the porch to his room.

"I'll set up the camera while you change. Meet you at the barn."

Alex's gear consisted of a stout aluminum tripod and a reinforced camera case containing the view camera, several lenses, and twelve flat film packs, each holding two exposures of four-by-five-inch film. The section of the barn he planned to use had no door, only a series of short boards nailed to the log wall as kind of ladder that led to an open upper wall. A similarly crude ladder descended the inside. He lugged the tripod and camera case up and over the wall in separate trips.

Alex was still adjusting the tripod when he heard Jacobo's heavy tread outside in the corral.

"Alex, where are you?"

"In here."

The old man pants as he pulls himself up the outside wall. Alex sees hands appear and grip the topmost log. Then the top of Jacobo's head peering over the wall, like Kilroy.

"You choose the hardest barn to get in."

"But it is cool in here. You'll like it."

A cane is thrown over the wall and lands in the hay, narrowly missing the camera. Then another arcs into the barn.

Jacobo pulls himself up two more steps and swings a leg over. His shirt is clean and pressed, but Alex notes with horror that it is vertically striped. He fears it will resonate too much with the vertical bars of light inside the barn and kill the picture. It is a shirt he has never seen before, and compared to the simple work shirts the old man wears almost every day, it seems uncharacteristic. Alex figures it was far back in Jacobo's closet, forgotten until now. He considers whether there is a polite way he can ask the old man to change his shirt again, then dismisses the thought. There isn't.

Jacobo climbs down into the barn. Alex hands him the canes.

"Well?"

"Go over there, old man, and sit on that bale." Alex points to a single bale in the corner where two walls of hay reach to the roof. An ancient pitchfork, patinaed with use, is stabbed into the bale.

"Should I bring these?" Jacobo holds up his canes.

"Yes."

Alex asks him to position himself so that one of the bars of light is centered on his face. Jacobo is uncertain just where the light is striking him and gets cross-eyed trying to see the light on his nose. He struggles a few minutes to align himself with the light.

Alex meanwhile is taking a light reading. He calculates broadly how the variables of exposure and development might interact. For this scene, with both deep shadows and bright streaks of light, he chooses to overexpose and, later, underdevelop the negative, in hopes of capturing detail in all areas of the picture.

Alex leans under the black camera hood and focuses. Then steps out and inserts a two-sided film pack. He asks Jacobo to hold both canes together, removes the light shield, and says, "Jacobo, did you know you look like a prisoner with those shadows and bars on you?" Jacobo winces at the idea, and Alex presses the cable release. He quickly replaces the light shield, removes the film pack, checks the focus, and flips and reinserts the film. Now he is ready to shoot again. He will shoot seven more times.

He says, "Let's try one standing up, with the pitchfork."

They talk little as the session proceeds. In a low, calm voice Alex gives the briefest instructions: sit, stand, look at me, look away. The moments when he changes film are empty. He fills one by asking, "Did you ever see the light this way? In bars?" but never hears the answer. He converses as though on autopilot. All of his concentration is on what he sees as he watches for the elements of the picture to converge. He waits for the weight to shift, the hand to relax, a cloud to pass the sun, then says, "That's good, Jacobo. Hold there."

He waits for the inevitable, and he waits for the ineffable. Soon or late, Jacobo will strike a posture or an expression that will cause the picture, in Alex's word, to "gel," and in a reflex, faster than thought, he presses the cable release.

In the session's first and third photographs, Jacobo is sitting; in number two he is standing, and in all three the bars of light that fall upon him look distractingly like suspenders. There is nothing otherwise striking about the pictures, but they do show that the vertically striped shirt, if anything, is an asset to the scene, and that it also makes a kind of statement. It is frayed and nappy across the stomach, as though many rough and heavy loads—hay bales, most likely—had been carried there. The tattered condition of the shirt, together with the dirty sneakers and the rough and swollen hands, says that this is a man of simple conditions. He has not known power, influence, or affluence. Here is a worker, not a boss.

In the fourth photograph, Jacobo again sits on the bale, leaning alertly forward, his canes held lightly in front of him. It is a pensive, intriguing pose except that a shaft of light burns brightly on the top of his head, like a collapsed halo.

Then Alex asks Jacobo to rise and put a foot on the bale he had been sitting on. The old man stands, then leans, half-sitting, against other bales behind him. In the fifth photograph he holds the pitchfork in one hand, a cane in the other, and the second cane, placed on the bale, leans against his chest. The photograph is cluttered with too many stick-like things. Jacobo looks like a juggler.

In the sixth he has put down one cane. It lies flat on the bale. He smiles, and the light on his face is good. Alex must have sensed he was getting close.

In the seventh the pitchfork is placed to the side. Jacobo holds both canes by the handle. He smiles. The picture is good, but lacks tension, a sense of drama, although Alex could not have known it at the time.

In the eighth Jacobo holds the canes against his body, grasping them lightly. The nearby pitchfork and the canes match the angle of the light, which splashes strongly down his face and chest. He frowns slightly. Does he frown because of the length of the session? Or because of the bold, serious light that glares across his eye? For an instant he looks fierce, even defiant. For an instant his face shows a certain power, a power that comes from long-tested tenacity and endurance. For an instant his self-possession is complete; no king could look more regal, no commoner more rooted in place, and in that instant, the shutter opens and closes.

12

River of Traps

Nothing so teaches respect for land and weather as the mountains in winter. Snow descends, binding field and forest in a numbing embrace. The stark, overexposed days ebb to dusk before they fairly begin, then yield to brittle nights. Storms the size of continents roll in and grind themselves to powder against the peaks, leaving the slopes as white as bone and colder than the insides of stones.

Eventually the peaks and sky reemerge, bluer than before, and high-altitude winds blow snow plumes a mile or more into space. From the valley, storm by storm, you watch cornices of snow build along the high divides, and once or twice, you might notice a break in the cornice where an avalanche has crashed free. Winter, silent and destructive, is also alluring, a seductress in ermine. You feel its pull in the dangerous cold, in the spectacle of the inviting, impassable land. There is so much to be known, yet so little you directly sense. The soul of the mountain winter is the avalanche you never heard.

For Anne and me the threat inherent in the land was invigorating. It made our actions more significant, our mistakes more consequential. The mired axle, the dead battery, the slip in the river truly mattered in winter. We lived with a sharper sense of our mettle, as though it were a muscle we could feel.

As luck had it, the winter we moved into our cramped new house was especially severe. The temperature had fallen well below zero on the morning, past Christmas, when we applied the top coat of plaster to the interior walls. A half-dozen friends came to mix and haul and trowel. Kerosene heaters blasted like jets through the day to keep our water barrels—and ourselves—from freezing.

On the tenth of January we moved in. On the fifteenth, snow began to fall, and intermittently it continued, every day but two, for the rest of the month. By the first of February snow was three feet deep in the full sun of the open pasture. We had not yet fenced the house from the rest of the field, and our three horses, like all horses in the village, had no shelter but the trees. They lurked all day about the windows, staring in, watching us, hoping that our next move would take us to the corral where the hay was stored. The horses grew jittery in proportion to their hunger and cold. Snow falling from an eave sent them galloping in panic, kicking up clouds of powder. On an unheard cue, like starlings, they wheeled in perfect unison, then froze motionless, eyes wide, ears forward, staring toward the vanished thing that frightened them. We fed them at dawn and sundown, but they seemed never to rest. At night we woke to hear their heavy tread shudder the frozen ground, as they stalked behind the house like dream shapes, seeking shelter by the walls.

For a month and a half, the road to the house was blocked with snow. Since we had no well or plumbing, we packed in drinking water along with groceries. Sometimes we skied to the house with loaded backpacks; sometimes we slung goods across the back of a horse. Since the ditch was dry through the coldest months, we hauled wash water bucket by bucket from the river, where to our surprise, the flow beneath the shelves of ice bore a heavy load of silt.

The hard weather made hermits of us all. Alex and Susan were in the East, where Alex was teaching and Susan was working in the intensive care ward of a large hospital. We saw Jacobo and Liza more often than we saw anyone else. The old man had long since split and stacked his firewood. He fed his cows twice a day and shoveled out from each new snowfall. There was little else for him to do. The snowpacked village road and the pain of his arthritis kept him from his usual circuit of visits, so he spent his days at home, indoors, across the kitchen from a squat cast-iron woodstove that bore the name FATSO in raised capitals on the firebox.

"*¿Jacobo, que está haciendo?* What's happening?"

"Just burning wood. *No más que quemando leña.*"

We often showered or fixed dinner at Alex's house, where we made fires every evening to keep the plants and pipes from freezing. Later, on the starlit walk down the road we usually stopped at Jacobo and Liza's.

We talked first of the cold, which bore talking about since the nighttime low never crept above zero all January. And we also talked of the loggers who had come to the village, parking their campers and trailers at Tomás's station, to harvest a Forest Service sale of close to twelve million board feet of timber—a large one for the area. The sale was concentrated in our watershed, and the loggers had been hard at work since summer. Tomás's business thrived. He sold gas and snacks as never before and soon offered a full line of truck tires. Jacobo told us that Tomás had now also ordered a pair of pool tables, and daily waited their delivery.

The loggers started high and worked to lower altitudes as winter advanced. By the time we moved into our house, they were cutting the pine atop the ridge across from Jacobo's farm and ours. We watched the horizon of solid forest become a ragged line of individual trees. Our daily

chores were punctuated by the sound of chain saws and crashing pon-
derosas, and at night from our bed we could see the work light of the log
picker, bright as a planet, as it loaded the trucks that hauled the logs away
on frozen forest roads and empty highways while the rest of the world
slept.

The ceaseless felling of trees disturbed us. We wondered, for instance,
if the silt in the river were due to road building and log skidding, but we
did not mention these thoughts to Jacobo. The old man had worked many
winters cutting ties and squaring them by hand with axe and adze. He
had no special sympathy for trees. News of the logging operation brought
forth his own stories about the sawmill his brother had operated. And
word of the loggers' rowdy amusements reminded him of his younger
days as a bootlegger, the classic backwoods entrepreneur.

In the early years of his marriage, he said, he made whiskey from a still
beside the kitchen woodstove in the small house where he and Liza lived,
which stood near his brother's sawmill in a side canyon down the road
from his parents. He cooked mash in a copper kettle and condensed the
liquor in a coil that dripped into a drum. When there was a dance in
Peñasco or another nearby village, he filled Coke bottles and fruit jars
with moonshine and packed them in his saddlebags. He rode by forest
trails to the big, low-ceilinged *salas de baile* where the dances were held.
He rarely went inside but stayed by the door to sell his whiskey to the
thirsty, exhilarated dancers who came out to him. A bottle cost two bits, a
jar half a dollar. He was careful to sample his wares with restraint,
drinking, he said, "not too much, just enough to be friendly with the
customers."

"Did you drink it too, Liza?"

"No, I never touch it. But I could cook it, and I always knew when it
was done, because you take a few drops and put a match to it, and *poof!*—
like gasoline it went, and it smelled that way too." She crinkled her
nose—the way she must have, girlishly, a half-century ago. "I don't want
anything that smells like that."

"But you helped make it, so you are outlaws, both of you."

"Yes, outlaws," said Jacobo. "We are crooked, but not too dangerous."

"And never got caught?"

"Well, they try to catch us one day. The agents came to arrest me, but a neighbor comes ahead of them on the road and gives us the warning. We were living by the sawmill, and my parents were living here. But my parents were not home, and so we lock up our house tight, so it looked like no one lived there, and we come down here. The agents go first to our house, but they find nobody and can't see through the window if there is a still inside, so next they come here, looking for me:

"We hear 'knock knock' on the door.

"'Yes?'

"'Are you Jacobo Romero?'

"'I am,' I say.

"'Is this your house?'

"'It is,' I say. And they seem to believe me.

"And they look around but they find no still, no bottles, no corn, and they seem to get very mad that they find nothing, but they don't say so. And finally they go away, and don't come back. And we go back to our house like nothing happened."

"But those agents scared you, old man." Liza corrects him. "You don't want to go to prison."

"No I don't, and so we don't make much whiskey after that," he admits. "And that was too bad because it was pretty good whiskey, and I like the dances." He sips the last of his coffee, puts down the cup. "Yes, outlaws. We were crooked, but not so crooked anymore. Just farmers now. Old ones."

"Maybe still a little crooked," we tease him. "Maybe you know that *ladrón* who used to steal the water."

"*¡Hijolé!*" He covers his grin with a thick hand. "If I find that son of a bitchy I gonna hit 'em with the shovel!"

"Well, don't hit 'em tonight, 'cause no water is running and we've got to go," I say. "It is late." We excuse ourselves. Coatless, Jacobo accompanies us into the bitter cold, as his exacting sense of hospitality requires, to walk us the length of the porch to the picket gate. The snow creaks beneath our boots as we step into the road. We pause a moment to gaze upward. The Milky Way is as lustrous as the moon. Jacobo looks up too.

"Gonna be *frío* tonight. No clouds."

"*Sí, frío.*"

"*Buenas noches*, Jacobo."

"Buenas noches." The old man watches as we trudge into the gleaming night. Suddenly a pack of coyotes begins to yip across the river. Their voices echo, hard as metal, throughout the valley.

We saw more coyotes than people that winter. Most often we saw them in the pasture in early morning, hunting gophers beneath the snow. The gophers made their winter tunnels at the surface of the soil, relying on the snow to protect them from predators. The coyotes pursued them by plunging into the snow at intervals, snuffling about, then coming up for air and clearing their noses with a snort. They moved in high leaps, legs and toes elegantly pointed, pouncing from spot to spot. Striking a scent, they plunged more rapidly, even frantically, diving headlong into the snow. At last a coyote would rear back, head high, gopher wriggling in its jaws. Meticulously, like a sword swallower, the coyote crushed the ribs and choked the rodent down.

Near any other home in the valley coyotes were shot on sight, but Anne and I liked watching them and enjoyed their maniacal songs. Their coats were full and gray, yielding to rust on the legs and behind the ears. When they stood immobile against the arroyo tangle of willow and oak, they became invisible, seeming to melt away before our eyes. Their trails led in and out of the canyon mouth, where they chorused every night, and frequently we noticed their scat on the paths that led from our house to the corral and to the woodpile. Their spoor showed that in the spare weeks of February they subsisted mainly on juniper berries and grasses, plus occasional cats and gophers.

By mid-March, snow had melted from the south-sloping fields. The snowpack in the hills had compacted and afforded the coyotes better passage through the forest. They came less often to our land. Other, newer arrivals took their place.

Toward the end of the month a flock of Clark's nutcrackers took up residence in the cottonwoods by the river. And hawks arrived too. I lay on the bed after lunch one day, gazing out the window. Suddenly a dark shape plunged from the sky into the arroyo. Moments later, it reappeared, rising on a gust. It was a red-tailed hawk clutching a thin snake. The hawk sailed on the wind, unhurried, cargo writhing in its grasp.

On March thirtieth the first turkey vultures appeared. On the thirty-first we heard the year's first thunder. It hailed for several hours. I wrote in my journal, "Last thing we need is more wet. Danger very great for melt-time floods."

April brought more firsts. The first scolding by a chipmunk, the first swallows, and the first outdoor shower, a chilly one, rigged from a fifty-gallon drum set above a fire. The hot water siphoned across the top of the field through a garden hose. We used a shipping pallet for a deck in the bottom of the arroyo, and the water hissed through a lawn sprinkler hung in an apple tree.

We had water again because the ditch was full. A week earlier I'd joined other members of the ditch association and a half-dozen hired *peones* to clean the ditch of leaves, rocks, and accumulated muck and sand. It was hard, pick-and-shovel labor. Jacobo was represented in the effort by a grandson and two other teenagers, each of whom he paid sixteen dollars for the day. With the cleaning done, Tomás, as *mayordomo*, opened the head gate and declared the water available to anyone who wanted it. Only Jacobo did. Soon all his fields were sheeted with water. After a day or two he told me, "I am leaving a little in the ditch for you, in case you want to irrigate."

It was more a test than an invitation. Reluctantly, I put a board in the *presita* and sent the water to the field. I was still setting the *regadera* when snow began to fall. It fell, off and on, for four days, pushed by a biting wind. The storm shoved us back into winter, dumping a foot of muddy slush. Then came the year's first death.

On the eleventh of April Tomás's mother Claudiña died. Anne and I had known her as a shy woman, but warm and generous. There was no formal summoning of gravediggers to the cemetery. Word simply passed when the work would be done, and at the appointed hour eight or ten men gathered at the graveyard, each with a shovel or pick. Only one of us at a time could work in the hole, and we waited our turns as a cold drizzle fell.

The week following the funeral brought unseasonal thunderstorms. I walked up the river every morning and fed Tomás's cows for him. Each day the river rose, and was soon too deep to wade across. It carried away the logs we used for a footbridge between our land and the Americanos'. We found them some distance downstream and retrieved them, later installing them anew on stacks of sandbags. The river churned with

stumps and branches. We expected it to tear away the fence at the canyon mouth. It was now as brown as a bayou, but violent. Its old voice was gone and it raised an angry snarl, like race cars around a track. Even inside the house with the door closed, we heard the constant growl.

All that week the river haunted us, arguing with its banks, running chocolate and debris-choked, four or five times its normal size. But the fence held, and in time the flow slackened. We began to enjoy the outdoors again and lingered by the ford where the cows and horses liked to cross. The meadow there was the prettiest part of our land. The cows cropped the bluegrass so that it looked mown, and the tallest of our cottonwoods leaned overhead.

A year and a half earlier Anne and I had left the village to be married at my parents' home in Maryland. When we left on our wedding trip,

Jacobo and other neighbors had cautioned, "Don't leave all your fiesta back there, save some for El Valle."

As soon as we returned, we bought a lamb from Filiberto, butchered it, and invited everyone in the village to a barbecue beside the river. We built a circle of river cobbles for a fireplace and lashed juniper poles between the cottonwoods for racks to bear the roast corn, salads, and coolers of beer. Stumps and logs drawn up for seating completed the furnishings of our reception place, and long after the party ended, the meadow rang for us with laughter and familiar voices.

By May the river meadow was as green as on the day of the barbecue. We groomed the horses there, pulling winter hair from their backs by handfuls, which the birds scavenged for their nests. The valley filled with the shrieks and drumming of woodpeckers, and swallows reappeared for the first time since the April snow. On rocky outcrops by the canyon mouth clumps of pincushion cactus, called Mexicans' balls by Indians and Indians' balls by Mexicans, erupted in magenta blooms. These first flowers echoed winter's hardship, for they attracted their pollinators, the blow flies, with a smell like carrion.

May was good for birds and flowers, bad for cattle. On successive days I helped Tomás and Jacobo bring their cattle to Jacobo's corral, which had a chute, the best in the village, equipped with a kind of guillotine of two-by-fours that was strong enough to immobilize a bull. We forced the animals one by one through the chute, not holding back our whips and clubs, and trapped them in the guillotine, where I shot hypos of red-water vaccine into their necks. We also cut off the horns of the yearlings, which then ran from the chute with jets of blood pulsing from the stumps. Last, we turned to the calves, roping them head and heel and stretching them out in the dirt of the corral. We shoved a foreleg in the loop of the head rope to be sure the calf did not strangle. Then penknife in hand, Tomás did surgery, while Jacobo and I held tight the ropes on snubbing posts.

Tomás cut notches from the ears of each calf and castrated the bulls. He threw the severed testicles in the dust and poured a slug of kerosene as disinfectant into the open scrotum. Then he took a hot brand from the pitchwood fire and pressed it to the animal's ribs. A smoke of charred hair and flesh sizzled from the iron. The animals' bawling drowned out the sound of the river. When we finished and turned the herd out the gate, the corral was littered with discarded horns and bits of flesh, and every surface was slippery with panic-splattered cowshit.

"Good thing cows are pretty stupid," Jacobo observed as we left the corral.

"Why is that, Jacobo?"

"Because if they know better, they might try to kill us."

Days later, an unexpected storm dumped heavy snow throughout the mountains. Frost killed the apricot blossoms. The newspapers and radio reported that flood preparations were under way in towns and counties throughout the region. The cold spring had delayed the mountain runoff and kept adding to the high country's snowpack, which already was yards deeper than normal. The Indians at Taos filled hundreds of sandbags, building high the banks of Taos Creek where it ran through the pueblo. Residents of Embudo and Velarde, close beside the Rio Grande, moved their livestock and belongings to higher ground. Everyone waited with apprehension for warm weather to arrive.

The cottonwoods were in leaf and all the valley decked in green, when, precisely at noon on the twentieth of May, according to my journal, the rains began. Shortly before sunset I donned a slicker and walked to the bottom of the pasture. The river was already rising.

Within a day it reached the level it had attained in April, and then held steady. Blue skies returned for two days during which Alex and Susan Norton returned from their winter in the East. We prayed for clear weather to continue, but soon, heavy clouds again rolled in. It began to pour.

The rain on our roof, usually restful, now sounded like gravel pouring from a dump truck. I ventured out once, swathed in multiple ponchos, to fetch my horse, which was grazing on the far side of the river. I figured to have him closer to hand, before the rising river put him out of reach.

But the river, already too high and fast to wade, had again swept our footbridge from its mooring. It was a continuous rapids, foaming and chocolate, roaring from every standing wave. A heap of posts and wire, tangled with clots of rubbish, tumbled past in the current. I heard a

splash and saw chunks of turf fall from the bank into the swirl. And then heard a sound I could not recognize: a muted *clack*, hard and powerful like the steel-on-steel of trains coupling. I looked around and heard it again. It came from the river, from the bottom of the torrent. Then I realized it must be the sound of boulders, uprooted from the river bed, now rolling in the current and crashing, *clack, clack*, one against another.

A log spun by. A fencepost. Clods from the bank splashed into the current. I hurried upstream, hoping Jacobo's bridge was still in place.

Jacobo was at the crossing, maul in hand. He was pounding a stake the thickness of a fencepost into the ground. The river swirled around both ends of the bridge. Its waves splashed froth on the footboards.

"This bridge don't hold very much longer," shouted the old man. The river nearly drowned out his voice. "I got to tie him so he don't go down to Trampas."

We tethered the bridge to the stake with a pair of picket ropes. Jacobo had placed the stake so that when the bridge left its moorings, it would swing through the current and lodge in a quiet eddy against the bank.

He hid his maul and also the ax he had brought behind a cottonwood log a safe distance from the river. "No use to take them back," he said. "We gonna have plenty of work down here."

I said, "Jacobo, I better get my horse now or I won't be able to get him later."

"You better."

The bridge rocked under foot as I crossed. Jacobo waited while I caught the horse and bridled him. I rode back to the crossing, then clung to the animal's mane and fought him to try the current. Finally he lunged into the water and up the far bank. Rain fell in steady sheets as we trudged, leading the horse, up the fields.

I left Jacobo at his house and rode home as night fell, crossing the *acequia* where its waters ran through a culvert. They brimmed dangerously high. I realized that the valley's side canyons must be flooding, adding their waters to the ditch. Rain hammered on, punctuated by thunder, far into the night.

Anne and I awoke in the small hours to the sound of water gushing inside the house. We leapt from bed, afraid for the vulnerable adobes that bore the weight of the walls. Water was coursing somewhere under the raised floor of the kitchen.

We scrambled outside, and the faint beams of our flashlights showed a river of mud streaming down the road and spilling into the unfilled trench of the foundation. It surged into the house through a utility sleeve intended for future pipes. We scrambled to find rags and stuff them in the sleeve. My arm was in the water when the world blazed with lightning and thunder rocked the hill above us. The jolt ran up my arm and seemed to lift me off the ground.

"Get out of there, you fool!" Anne shouted.

I seized a shovel and tried to scrape a channel to divert the water from the house. But I could not move my arm, nor feel anything in it. Anne took the shovel from me and got the job done. Then we hurried up the road to the ditch.

We'd have made a ridiculous sight, had there been light enough to see, clad in rubber boots and sodden long johns, me ungainly with a useless arm, thrashing about the flooding ditch. We thrust thick poles, like giant plumber's helpers, into the plugged driveway culvert, prying with all our strength against the branches and detritus the current piled up. Water spewed from the ditch. Some of it streamed toward the house, but the greater part, a river of gravel and water, swept into the hayfield.

We churned with our poles, and at last the obstruction gave way; the culvert cleared. We limped back to the house, shivering yet comical, the butts of what seemed a spiteful joke.

Although by morning my arm was well again, the light of the new day did nothing to restore our humor. The flood from the ditch had deposited sand and gravel several inches deep over much of the hayfield. Only the tips of the spring grasses showed through the sludge.

Much worse was what we saw at the river.

A quarter of the meadow no longer existed. The land was gone, dissolved. Swept down the river. The fire ring of river cobbles, where we'd barbecued the lamb, was now a swirl of coffee-colored water. The bank that had tapered to the river was a broth of standing waves. We stared dumbly at the new scene. The land fell abruptly, vertically to the water, exposing a wall of black loam protected only by dangling roots. The mild splashes I'd heard the day before were now crashes as barrow-sized loads of soil parted from the meadow and plunged into the torrent. The main channel of the river surged where we had held the wedding feast, and flotsam bobbed in the slack water where the channel used to be.

In normal times, the Rio Trampas was a mere creek that meandered through meadows and woods. It gained river status the way a Kentuckian becomes a colonel. Where the real thing is scarce, substitutes are promoted.

But now the River of Traps was a real river. Yet it lived in the body of a creek. It made room for its new size by straightening its curves and grinding away the land. We stared at the torrent, hearing the *clack, clack* of boulders under the flow.

Upstream and downstream conditions were the same. Every bend in the river was cut raw, as the banks gave way and sod collapsed into the current. The water tore away the fence at the canyon mouth and ran in a turbulent sheet from one rocky wall to the other. But a ledge on our side remained clear, wide enough for Jacobo's cattle to wander down the canyon. Grateful for a mission, I went to tell the old man about the fence.

I found him by the river. His bridge had washed into the eddy, as he had planned, and he was securing it with extra ropes.

"Jacobo, what has happened! Did you ever see a flood like this before?"

"No. Never that I can remember." He gestured disgustedly toward opposite bank where the river gouged a scar. "*Años pasados*, we had high water, but I never seen the river cut so much."

"So what is different now?"

"*No sé.* Too much snow. Too much rain. *Es la mano de Dios.*"

Perhaps the hand of God lay behind the flood, but Jacobo was not resigned to it. Most of the damage to his land was on the far side of the river, where he could not attack it, but he came with me to see what might be done for our land by the canyon.

He surveyed the damage, then firmly but indirectly gave instructions: "If I were you," he began, "if this was my place, I would do two things. First, I don't pay attention to those cows. They got plenty of grass, and they don't bother anything for a while. Next, I put some cedars where the water is cutting, and maybe that will hold."

"Put cedars? How?"

"You need to cut plenty more stakes like the one we tie the bridge to, and drive them deep, along the bank. Then wire the cedars—or any kind of branches you can find—to the stakes and throw them in the water. The more green they got the better. You gonna see. It can help, I think."

"Branches can stop water like that?"

"They can."

"We can keep the bank from falling?"

"You can."

It took me a moment to absorb the idea, to realize we could fight the flood. Had I acted the day before when the first clods yielded to the flood, I might have saved the meadow.

Jacobo prodded, "You got a chain saw?"

"Yes."

"You got wire?"

"Yes."

"Well, go."

I collected tools: the maul, chain saw, hatchet, pliers. Jacobo left to check his own land. Alex was in Santa Fe that morning, but Anne came to help, as did Susan Norton and another friend from farther up the road. We cut a truckload of scrubby junipers from the hill behind the corral and gathered bushels of wire we'd saved from hay bales.

We cut and pounded and wired through the rest of the morning and into afternoon, spurred by the growl of the river and the dismal splashes of turf and soil plunging into the flood.

Soon our labors had an effect. As Jacobo instructed, we planted the stakes well back from the edge and bound the juniper tops to them with ropes of baling wire six or eight strands strong. One by one we threw them in. The dark water slammed the trees against the bank and sucked them down, fuming and seething through the foliage. Each new juniper stirred the water to a louder boil. Finally a forest of dwarf trees shielded the bank. The whole mass was anchored to a dozen or more stakes, each as thick as a man's arm, and intertwined with wires that ran in every direction. Now the voice of the river changed. Its roar gave way to a constant hiss, and the bank began to hold.

Wet, muddy, and spent, we watched the brown current test the juniper and saw the juniper prevail. Jacobo had been right. The main current was deflected from the bank. The torn sod ceased its retreat.

There was little more to do. Farther downstream along the meadow the river did not charge its banks as much as roll over them. The water spread broadly over an area marked by islands of willows and cottonwoods. Trees that had once leaned above the channel now toppled into the flow, their roots undercut. Huge jams of logs and ruined fencing pressed against them.

We were carrying our tools back to the truck when again we heard the ominous plash of crumbling river banks. But it was not our land; the juniper still held. It was the other side, the Americanos' side, where the current we'd deflected now drilled the earth and sliced it away. Too bad for them, but there was nothing we could do. We'd protected our land, and now we had to rest. We could not have crossed the river with our lives, let alone with saws and mauls and axes. The river, obedient to *la mano de Dios*, would do its work. Water ruled. Water would show.

That night it rained again. Hard. Anne and I speculated about how the

Americanos' land would look in the morning, and the image was never far from our minds of the tall banks disintegrating into darkness. But bone-tired, we slept selfishly, without worry. We had fought. We'd not won much; perhaps we were losing, but at least we had fought.

13

The Bird with the
Bleeding Throat

Early the next morning Anne and I walked down to the river. Alex joined us there. The river was running slightly lower than its peak of the day before, and the shield of juniper remained in place. Erosion continued on the opposite bank, but it now seemed measured and methodical, not savage as before. It was small consolation. The sight of the meadow, ripped open like a carcass on a hook, left us speechless with dismay.

Walls of raw earth, taller than a man and wetly oozing, boxed the torrent on both sides. The tops of the undercut banks drooped like wet hat brims, from which pieces tore and fell into the swirl. No wind stirred from the hills, but the turbulence of the river created a breeze. It wafted the pale roots dangling from the banks back and forth, like the tentacles of jellyfish.

A good portion of the meadow was now vanished and bound for Mexico or, more precisely, for the stinking flats behind one of the Rio Grande's dams. We felt as though part of us were washed away with it.

"You missed a show yesterday, Alex," I said.

"I can see that," he answered.

"It won't be the same again."

"No," he said. "It won't." Alex sounded tentative, a little guilty. I hoped he felt that way. He shouldn't have left the village the day before without seeing if he were needed.

"We sure busted our asses yesterday."

"It looks that way. Sorry I wasn't here."

"Me too." The words didn't come out right. I meant them to sound matter-of-fact. Instead they sounded pissed-off and whiny. I was angry at the river, angry at Alex, angry at myself. If I'd understood sooner how to fight the waters, more of the meadow might have been saved.

Alex walked off a little way and prodded one of the stakes with his foot. "The Americanos are getting it a lot worse than us." At that moment a ledge of sod broke from the opposite side and splashed into the current.

"Come on," said Anne. "Let's get out of here. We've got other places to be."

"Think I'll drive up the road and see how the river looks farther up," I said. "Any takers?"

No response.

"What do you say?"

"I've seen enough water for a while," Anne said.

"Maybe I'll do a little work down here," muttered Alex. "There are places that could use more juniper."

I made my way alone to the yellow truck.

The road out of the village climbed five miles beside the river, past the mouths of logging roads, newly smoothed and widened for the current operation, past Diamante where the forest opened briefly and the disintegrated ruins of Jacobo's childhood home rippled the surface of a field, and past tall outcrops of granite, spangled with lichens and marked by the dynamite that years ago had helped to build the road.

The river was as swollen in its higher reaches as it was lower down. In one place, road builders had pushed a wall of fill against the channel, but the river had reclaimed its path, swallowing the fill and half the road as well. Already the Forest Service had surrounded the washout with sawhorses and flashing amber lights.

Most astonishing were the springs bursting from the canyon sides. Even where the land had lain free of snow for weeks, water burbled from clefts and outcrops, from ledges and depressions, from under rotting stumps. The land leaked like a rain forest, from places where cactus normally grew. It was evident that groundwater, not surface run-off, was a main source of the flood. The mountain soils were saturated. They lay like a swollen sponge upon the bedrock, and wherever the sponge sagged or crimped, water burst through.

The higher I drove the clearer the water became. The road ended where a pack trail continued toward the peaks. Here, although the river was many times its normal size, it retained its usual crystalline clarity. No silt or color was in it. If the water was clean coming out of the wilderness, I wondered, why was it dark and destructive below?

Weather alone seemed an insufficient cause. If, as Jacobo said, no storms in memory had made the river so destructive, then it seemed likely some outside cause, some catalyst, had broken the balance of the watershed. Logging was an obvious culprit. Trucks, cats, and skidders had torn the skin of the watershed for a year. How could they not be responsible for the damage we suffered? The fact, which I discovered days later, that adjacent, unlogged watersheds escaped serious erosion, added to the proof.

But as I drove down the canyon, past scores of springs where none had been before, I had to admit that not all the evidence fit. I saw no surface run-off that might be blamed on the logging. Instead, the weakness of the system seemed to be the capacity of the soils to hold back rain and snow melt. How tree cutting and road building could have affected that, I could not see. More and more, because I could not explain what was happening, I felt the victim of the flood.

For a week it rained every afternoon and cleared the following morning. The river rose and fell in a daily rhythm but did not approach the heights it had before. Our routines returned almost to normal. One evening, in spite of a drizzle, I heard the song of a hermit thrush from the tall pines on the far side of the valley. The hermit thrush lives up to its name, for it is a reclusive bird, and rarely seen, but its song is a conspicuous sound of early summer. It sings in flute-like notes, ascending a scale as though asking a question, then falling as though in answer. Walt Whitman, in a poem about President Lincoln, once invoked the song as a refrain of grief and sorrow, a song, he called it, "of the bleeding throat." The refrain, languorously repeated, now lingered in the forest calm. I wondered what it signaled: grief for things past, or for things to come.

Jacobo announced it was time to get busy. Though the weather remained unsettled, he said we needed to repair the fence across the canyon mouth. His cattle had not tested the gap the flood had opened, but he reasoned that as the water dropped, they might. He sent Alex for metal fence posts and me for barbed wire, and we trucked our load of gear to the corner of the hay field, then lugged it the rest of the way. The old fence had spanned the river some thirty yards shy of the property line, and the portion that had not been washed away was in poor repair. We decided to build a new fence closer to the line, running seventy yards from an outcrop on the canyon side and across the river to a wall of rock on the other side. It took a day to beat the metal posts into the stony ground and run four strands of wire. We salvaged some cedar posts from the flood debris and built a gate in the fence, partly for our use, but also for the fishermen who wandered the stream—so they would not have to choose between climbing the fence and cutting it.

We strung the wire across the river at a narrowing of the channel, Alex having waded the current some distance upstream where the waters permitted. Jacobo offered a stream of advice as we threw equipment back and forth and pulled the wire across. This was our boundary fence, but Jacobo was no less vigilant than if it were his own. He closely watched the installation of the stays and tested every span of wire.

Tired and wet, we hauled our gear back to the truck as clouds gathered for another evening shower. Jacobo was quiet on the ride to the house. He had a habit, when something was on his mind, of grinding his gums together while staring intently ahead. It made him look as though he had lost a tiny object in his mouth and was trying to find it. As we drove along, he stared at the big field next to ours. It belonged to a widow named Victoria, who lived in Albuquerque. She rented the field to Tomás.

Jacobo ceased churning his jaws. "We took care of a problem today," he said. "Next we have to fix Victoria's."

Victoria's field fronted a portion of the Americanos' pasture along the river. The flood had ripped out the fence between the two properties.

"But that's Tomás's job," I said. "The fence is on his side of the river."

"No, I don't think Tomás is gonna do it. I think maybe we gonna have to."

Jacobo said no more, but I thought I understood his reasoning. He feared his cattle might pick their way across the river, where the grass was not only greener but taller. And the alfalfa was lush. That was the problem. Ordinarily it would have been Tomás's responsibility to repair the fence, but he knew—and Jacobo knew he knew—that because of the alfalfa, Jacobo would act first.

Spring alfalfa is too rich a food for cows whose digestion is attuned to dry, bland winter feed. A sudden bellyful of alfalfa causes terrible colic, and if the animal doesn't die outright, the usual treatment is to stab a hole through its side to relieve the bloat, and then butcher or sell it quickly before infection sets in.

Jacobo was determined to repair the fence before his cows could eat themselves to death. He described the project: "We only need to dig two holes, and probably we can find the posts right there. Then put the wire and some stays, and that is all."

"Why don't you use metal posts, like today? It'd be faster."

"Don't need 'em. The ground is not too rocky." Speed was less important than cheapness. Metal posts cost money, cedar only time.

"When do you expect to do this?" I asked, knowing the answer.

"Probably tomorrow. In the morning," he said.

Because of the flood, I was already far behind the schedule I'd set for writing. "I can't help you tomorrow," I said, already feeling guilty, "but probably the next day I can. Anyway, the river is still too high for the cows to cross. And it's gonna rain more tonight."

"Uh huh," he said, and his jaws started moving again, looking for the lost thing.

Alex rode in the back of the truck and missed our conversation. That night, in spite of steady rain, Jacobo walked to his house and laid out the matter to him. He asked more directly than he had asked me: "So, you think you can help me fix that fence?"

Alex thought about his own neglected work, about the disagreeable weather, about the lack of urgency, since days would pass before the river lowered enough for cattle to cross. He listened to the rain on the roof. "Yes," he said, "as soon as the weather clears, I'll give you a hand."

Jacobo thanked him and soon left. Rain drummed on the roof all night.

The next morning, about eight o'clock, the rain abated. Alex was heading to the darkroom, coffee in hand, when he heard the sound of Jacobo's canes on the porch. He opened the door for the old man, who wasted no time on pleasantries.

"We can fix that fence now," he said.

"It's going to rain again in a few minutes. Look at those clouds."

"No, no, those clouds are okay. They don't bother us. Let's go."

"It's going to rain."

"No, not too much."

"Really, Jacobo, we'd be wasting our time. The weather's no good."

"Well, if you don't want to work. . . ."

"It's not that. I want to work in a way that I can get something done."

"Well, that fence is something. Come on. Susan will let us use her truck."

Without waiting for reply, Jacobo turned and strode outside. He called over his shoulder, "I will wait for you out here."

Grumbling, Alex found his gloves and boots. He checked the Nikon and pocketed an extra roll of film, lest the day be a total waste.

They stopped first at Jacobo's for tools: a post hole digger, a roll of barbed wire, shovel, pliers, and an iron digging bar weighing forty pounds or more. If they waited for drier weather, they'd be able to drive the truck to the river and avoid lugging so much equipment. But a fence was down. And Jacobo would not rest.

They turned from the main road onto a mud-slick track that led to Victoria's gate. The truck wallowed side to side. The more Alex turned the wheel the less control he had. He doubted they could make the grade climbing out. The truck slid to a stop next to the ditch. "Hold on a minute Jacobo, let me see if I can turn this thing around."

"No that's all right. Let's get to work," the old man said and opened his door before Alex had shut off the engine.

Alex got out and looked at the mud-caked tires. The ruts they had made coming down the track were discouragingly deep. If he got the truck badly stuck, Susan would be furious. She needed the truck to get to work at the Española hospital later that afternoon. Probably he would have to put chains on. And he could only do that if he lay down in the mud. But the jack, he remembered, was back at the house. He looked at Jacobo. The old man, lifting tools from the back of the truck, wore a slight smile.

Alex carried the post hole digger and the iron bar on his shoulder, struggling to balance them. Jacobo put the pliers in his pocket and took up a shovel. They carried the spool of wire on a broken rake handle between them. With every step, as they marched down the field, the dangling camera slapped Alex in the side. The iron bar dug in his shoulder, and he lost his grip on one of handles of the post hole digger. He clung to the other with a single finger that felt as though it would break.

I was watching. From inside my house, across the arroyo, I could see them descending to the river. A new drizzle began to pop against the roof. I felt guilty for not helping but not guilty enough to leave the warmth of the house. The way I figured it, Alex deserved the job. Things evened out.

Alex and Jacobo had not been at the river ten minutes when the popping on the roof exploded in a roar. I looked out the window through a gray curtain of rain, and saw them, heads bent against the downpour, half-running to the truck. Now Alex's camera, exposed to the rain, slapped against the bar and the tool handles. Too bad for him, I thought. I was right to stay in.

They were soaked to the skin when they reached the truck. Alex cranked the engine. "Let's get out of here," he said hotly. "If we can!"

"It will stop soon."

"It's been raining a week. It will rain a week more!" Already moisture from their clothes and breath had misted the windows. Alex turned the defroster full blast and reached for the gear shift.

Jacobo put his hand on Alex's. "Let's wait a little longer," he said. There was a note of concern in his voice. He feared if Alex left, he would lose his *peón* for the day, and the fence would not be fixed. "We can stay five minutes, and see will the rain stop."

Alex shut off the engine. His silence was almost sullen. Jacobo wiped the mist from his window and peered out. "Do you know," he asked, "why they call this place by the turn in the road *la vuelta Sáles?*" Alex merely shook his head. "Used to be, there were three or four houses here. It was strange, the people then would build their houses on the hills, not on the flat, and you had to walk up many steps to reach the door. A man named Salazar—they called him Sáles—lived in a house right there by the turn and that is why they called it *la vuelta Sáles.* He was half-blind, and two old women who lived next to him were in the same bad shape. I used to visit them when I was young. They were a mother and a daughter, but both were so old they looked the same."

Jacobo noted that Alex was less restless now. He was beginning to show interest in the story. The old man's animation increased as he worked deeper into the tale.

"The mother was all blind, and the daughter, like Sáles, almost. She could see enough to walk up the road to visit neighbors by herself, but she said she was afraid of the dogs that barked at her along the way. . . ."

Rain pounded the roof. Jacobo gestured broadly, as though to an audience beyond the windshield. Alex noticed that the misted windows diffused the light in the truck. The Nikon was in his lap. He cocked it, adjusted the f-stop.

"Now, I had an uncle who was very mean. His name was Vidal, and he wanted to test how afraid this old lady really was—or if she was crying about the dogs just for sympathy. . . ."

Alex raises the camera. Jacobo looks at him.

"And so one day Vidal sees her coming. . . ."

The shutter clicks. The old man's smile tells what he's thinking: *Gotcha! You're not leaving now!*

"And Vidal makes his plan. The road was muddy, and to stay on the dry, the woman has to walk on the side, very close to a barn that was in the arroyo. Vidal hides by the corner of the barn, waiting for her. . . ."

Click.

"As the blind woman passes, he reaches out, under the skirts. He grabs her leg. Pinches hard. He goes '*rarr, rarr,*' growling, mean!"

Click again.

"She screams! She cannot see what it is. She screams loud. Vidal feels warm water all over his hand. Ha! She is pissing! Ha!"

Jacobo laughs too hard to speak. Click.

"Vidal runs behind the barn before she can tell if it is a dog or a man. She keeps screaming."

Click.

"Ha! But Vidal got his pay: he has her piss on his hand and all up his arm. Ha!"

Click.

The rain drums on, and the stories continue: Vidal is a layabed; he

feigns sickness to cadge sickbed foods like *atole* and powdered *carne seca* from his wife. He persuades her to feed him spoonful by spoonful, but she is too slow. Suddenly Vidal leaps up, grabs the bowl, and wolfs down the food.

Another time Vidal lies to an old man about the old man's son. The son had gone *'fuera*—outside the village—to the sheep camps, and the man had no news of him. Vidal gallops to the man's house. His horse is lathered. He is out of breath. He seems consoling. He says to the old man, "Your son is dead!" Then weeps with him, despondently. Then off rides Vidal, laughing now to himself. He indeed had no news of the young man, but was only making trouble.

At last one night Vidal is drunk and receives his comeuppance. Jacobo's father Narciso convinces him that a glimmer by the ditch—a tree whose wet bark gleamed in the moonlight—is actually a witch. Taunted by Narciso, Vidal boasts that he will capture the witch. He puts on his

clothes inside out—which everyone believed protected you from sorcery—and sallies forth. He runs from the house, lunges across the ditch, and dives into a stump!

It has rained for an hour, but finally the shower eases. Jacobo and Alex, warmed by the stories, step out into momentary sun. They stretch, shake out their jackets, and put on their gloves. Laden once more with tools, they head down the field to the river. Alex has his pictures. Jacobo has his *peón*. It will not be long before the fence is repaired.

And then the rains return.

I am finishing my lunch when I see them come back from the river. Soon afterward, rain lashes the windows and roars upon the roof. It lasts throughout the afternoon.

At supper Anne asks, "Do you hear a difference in the river? I think it's louder."

We listen a while. A drizzle patters on the roof. The refrigerator hums. The dog whimpers in a dream. Behind these sounds rises the guttural quarrel of the river. It penetrates the closed door, the adobe walls, the rain-streaked windows. For weeks it has been an uninvited guest who will not leave. As I listen now, the sound of the river does *seem* stronger, and perhaps meaner, but is it really louder, or is it amplified by my fear that it might be?

"I don't know," I say. "I hope you're wrong, but I better go down and see."

The dog follows me across the hayfield but balks at the gate to the river. The water's roar is a nearly physical barrier. Descending the slope to the meadow is like stepping through the door of a factory, into the din of furnaces and engines. Even in my thoughts, I have to shout.

The water is at least as high as the peak of the first flood—and rising. It has undercut several of the stakes that tethered junipers to the riverbank. A section of them, the entire upstream half, is held by one wire rope. It threatens to tear away.

At that moment Anne appears at the hayfield fence. I shout to her to bring ropes from the house. An instant later the last stake pulls free. I grab it but am nearly yanked into the current. I let go and the great mass of brush it had anchored speeds through the rapids and lodges on a gravel bar.

Two weeks earlier that bar had been the bank of the river. Now it marks the middle, with rapids seething on either side. The raft of brush that has snagged on it is now the most valuable thing in the valley. Our supply of materials by the river is otherwise exhausted. Collecting more would cost time—and land. Already, the naked bank, where the brush tore away, is dissolving in the torrent. Chunks of earth as large as hay bales splash into the roiling water. Our land, yard by yard, is vanishing.

At last Anne arrives, breathless from running, with a long picket rope. We tie one end to a stake upstream of the gravel bar. With the other end around my waist I wade into the main channel, fearful of the clacking boulders that roll unseen beside me. The rope tightens as the current rises past my hips and pushes me downstream. Angling sideways, weight against the rope, I can inch across the flood. I reach the relative safety of the bar and take off the rope, which I tie to the snagged heap of brush and branches.

Hand over hand, I follow the rope back to the bank. We untie it from the stake, which we know cannot hold against both the brush and the current. Then together we heave on the line. Nothing moves. We heave again, with all our strength. The raft of brush teeters, then topples into the flood. It speeds downstream like a runaway horse, pulling us behind it. We run to keep up, leaning against the rope to coax the wired-up jumble to the bank. At last we beach it in an eddy and scramble to take it apart.

We need more tools. Anne runs for the chain saw and the maul. I drag the brush, section by section, to the fast eroding bank. It is raining hard now, a cold rain, and every garment I am wearing is drenched. The light, too, is failing, as angry clouds screen the low sun.

Anne returns. I yank the chain saw to life and cut the picnic counter from our wedding feast into a dozen new stakes. We work maniacally—to warm ourselves as well as save the land. We are like peasants fighting the Yangtze. We are in the river, mud-slick to the hips. We are out of it, lashed by rain. We cut, haul, chop, and pound. We bind and heave. My shivering makes it hard to use the pliers. The heads of the stakes dance as I pound them. Now the voice of the river changes, rising in complaint as a new wall of brush builds against the bank. Anne's wrist is bleeding from a wire cut. The boulders' clack is answered by the thud of the maul. We exhaust our supply of tops and brush. My hands shake so much I cannot tie the wire to the final stake. Anne must do it for me.

We can scarcely see but the bank seems to hold. Night is on us. We can do no more. We trudge up the field, mindless as mules, saving enough thought, we hope, to be able to kindle fire in the woodstove.

By morning the river has washed out the new fence at the canyon. It has swept away all of the brush along our bank, except what we re-staked in desperation the night before. The river is carving a shortcut across the point of land where we used to camp and cook. On our way to fetch more baling wire and tools, we meet Jacobo. He tells us disgustedly that the fence he and Alex built the day before has been destroyed.

We return to work, and Alex and Susan join us, cutting branches, twisting wires, and pounding stakes. The river has felled a tall cottonwood on the Americanos' side. It's a mother lode of branches and logs, but we can't get to it. The river has also sluiced away a point of land where the Americanos planned to build a road and bridge, and it has toppled a bushy, half-dead juniper that grew there. We scavenge the juniper and throw its pieces, tethered with wire, into the torrent.

We notice, as our work progresses, that our efforts focus the current more forcefully on the Americanos' side. Now we no longer hear the sound of collapsing banks from underfoot. It comes to us from across the din of the river.

For two days we continue the fight. Then the river begins to subside. We learn there is not much damage in the upper half of the valley. The worst is in our stretch. Across from us, the Americanos have lost a good portion of their most beautiful and useful land. Upstream, opposite Victoria's, an even bigger chunk of their meadow has been washed away. Near the fence that Jacobo and Alex temporarily repaired, the widow's land now drops in thirty-foot cliffs to the river. Nor has Jacobo been spared. Like us, he presides over long new stretches of river sand and cobbles, where meadow used to be.

The damage is done, the crisis over. Suddenly there is no urgent work at hand. We return to ordinary things, but approach them numbly. I stay inside at my desk, writing nothing. The exhaustion that lingers from our battle with the river will not go away. A feeling of depression hangs in the air like the uncommon humidity rising from the land. We scarcely try to fight it.

Days pass. Maybe a week goes by. I don't go down to the river. One morning I hear the hermit thrush singing again from the pines across the valley. I stand on the porch and feel the sun, full and warm. The youngest of our horses canters across the far pasture, tail high. I can barely see him through the cottonwoods, which seem intensely green. Then it dawns on me that the rains have brought a rare florescence to the land.

The orchard grass is shooting up without irrigation. Patches of yellow hymenoxys, as sunny as daisies, paint the gravel hills. Blue penstemon decorates the road cut, and its scarlet cousin laces the arroyo. Lupine and wild pea tangle along the *acequia*, and there are red locoweeds that dry blue and primroses with tissue-thin petals that wilt in the sun. There is paintbrush by the woodpile, and sweet clover, yellow and white, along the road. By the end of June, the river is still high by normal standards, but we can cross it again. The land is lush. We repair the fences. The routines of the growing season guide us from morning to night. Down by the river, the cottony seeds of the *alamos* drift in the breeze and cover the wounded meadow like gauze.

Fence Canto

Life is fences.

Anyway, for a cow.

Was a cow and a calf in different pastures. They cry to each other all day. Cow in one fence, calf in the other, but the cow don't know where the calf got out, and the calf don't know to remember. All day he cry, getting hungry.

Calf got to learn about fences. Got to know he gonna spend his life inside them. The cow knows. She been all her years inside some fence, waiting for the open gate.

One day the gate is down. She goes in the road. Through the gate she goes, head low, swinging side to side. "Who is there?" she is asking. The people are there. To put her in the corral, in the chute, to give shots for red water, to spray the lice, to cut the horns and ears of her calf.

Maybe after that she go back mad to the pasture and want to get out. She make a hole in the fence. We don't let her do that. Back to the corral with that cow, and we hit her hard to get her in the chute.

Then we put her the cross. We call it cross, la cruz, *but it is a* Y. *It goes at the throat and we tie it with wire on her neck. We use a cedar branch that makes a fork, a strong one, plenty heavy. She don't like it, but it don't come off and now she break no more fences.*

Like in the Book, now she got to bear her cross, waiting and waiting for the open gate.

But the fence don't last forever. Wire got to break, posts got to rot.

Like this barn, always leaning, leaning. You don't know when it gonna fall down, but it will. Like this man, he is leaning too. Leaning on his little sticks because his posts are rotten like the barn. Maybe he gonna fall down tomorrow. Only thing can hold a barn on rotten posts is God.

Same thing for the man.

14

Preparation

There is a bird that lives along the Río Trampas known as the dipper. Smaller than a robin, it behaves like a fish, for it never leaves the ribbon of stream in which it lives. Even in the depths of winter when the river is bridged with ice, it spends much of its time not just in the water, but under it. The dipper subsists, the year around, on the larvae of aquatic insects—caddis flies, mayflies, and the like. Perhaps because of its diet, the dipper has the brain of a trout.

Although it flies with speed and agility, the dipper uses its aerial skill in two directions only: upstream and downstream. Where the river bends languidly around some point of land, the dipper will not fly the shortcut; without exception, it follows the bend. Nearly all its flying is done within a few feet, or even inches, of the river's surface, as though its internal compass functioned only within a wingspan or two of moving water. The dipper skims along, skinny wingtips beating fast and shallowly, like a fish's tail. You walk down to the water, and as the trout dart for cover, the bird flees too. It calls an alarm, like spare change rattled in a jar, and its lead-gray shape quivers out of sight.

If you follow where the shape has disappeared, you will see the bird again. It will have lighted on a boulder streaked white from previous visits. There the dipper studies the river and soon commences, with no sense of dignity or grace, to squat deeply and then stand up, squat and stand, and squat and stand again. These "dipping" exercises, which give the bird its name, continue until the dipper steps into the stream to stroll underwater, pecking at larvae. Moments later the bird resurfaces a yard or two away, and bobs through the rapids like a fat cork, soon to scramble out on another white-stained rock to squat and stand again.

Although eccentric, the dipper possesses a number of admirable qualities, at least from an anthropocentric point of view. It is fervently loyal to its two-or-three-hundred-yard stretch of territory, seldom migrating more than a mile downstream in winter and sometimes not migrating at all. It also tends to be loyal to its mate, with whom it builds a nest well hidden beneath an overhang in the riverbank. Dippers are social birds, but not gregarious. The mate is company enough. Regardless of season, you find them usually in pairs, one not far upstream of the other, and if you see a single where you are used to seeing two, you may persuade yourself, sadly, that the bird trills for a mate it will not see again.

I admired the dipper for its tenacity and delighted in encountering it on walks by the river, but my ideas about it slowly changed. Eventually the bird came to symbolize for me a persistent danger. Imagine a map of the dipper's world. It would show a realm fifty feet wide by a thousand long, studded with intimately known rocks and eddies and fallen trees. To either side of the skinny homeland lies an infinite *terra incognita*, a wilderness unacknowledged and unexplored. I worried, and so did Anne, that the village was becoming for us like the dipper's patch of stream, that we were beginning to mistake the familiar horizons of the valley for those of the world.

There were hazards in village life, which few of our neighbors, with the notable exception of Jacobo and his family, seemed able to escape. In spite of decades of turbulent dealings with Efrén Chacón and others, Jacobo had retired from quarreling, much as he had retired from "the sheeps." In old age he watched impartially as the disagreements of others ripened into grudges, and grudges into feuds, even to the point of violence. Especially in the dark, cabin-fevered days of winter, some of us dwelled too much on the foibles of other families up and down the road. It was a weakness without prejudice. Anglos and Hispanos seemed equally vulnerable to the addiction of critical gossip and the negativity that grew from it. We ourselves were not immune.

Alex, fortunately, had access to an antidote: travel. Over the years he developed an arrangement with Duke University that enabled him to teach for part of the year in North Carolina and spend the remaining months at home in the village. All things considered, he seemed to have struck an enviable balance between two nearly opposite worlds. But Anne and I were neither so mobile nor so employable, though we wished to be. Increasingly, we thought of moving on, if only to gain skills marketable enough to return to the village in fuller control of our fates.

I was also feeling the tug of a more conventional kind of ambition than that which had brought me to the valley. Anne agreed that a change was due but never fooled herself into thinking that she wanted it. Not me. I believed I needed it. I had finished a draft of my book about the mountains, but it was a raw thing. I needed the resources of a research library to finish what I'd started. I wrote an application for a fellowship at the University of Texas, and I was tempted to say what was really on my mind: "I want to finish my book, and avoid the fate of a dipper." But I was circumspect, wrote other things, and was accepted. Anne and I made preparations to leave after the hay was in.

Jacobo was then also making preparations. Each year his arthritis grew more painful, especially in his knee. Worse, he developed the symptoms of congestive heart failure. Susan Norton was the first to notice. She arranged for a friend of hers, a doctor, to visit Jacobo at his home. Prescriptions and a follow-up visit ensued. Jacobo's heart condition was mild at first, but as time passed, the vials of pills atop the refrigerator multiplied. He was obliged to spend less time in the fields and more time at the house. He could afford to. His oldest son Lalo was home now, fulltime. He had retired from sheepherding and took over most of the farm duties.

Jacobo bought tortoise-shell reading glasses and passed many hours studying the Bible and the emphatic tracts that the Jehovah's Witnesses and other evangelicals left weekly at his house. At Liza's urging he gave up snuff and alcohol. He was never much of a drinker, but together we had all enjoyed the occasional beer or *whiskito*. Suddenly he swore off it, along with his beloved Copenhagen (though we heard rumors of snuff tins cached in trees and other secret places). Jacobo gave up these small pleasures without a murmur of regret. He said he was "getting ready."

Jacobo was much on our minds as the time for departure neared. Anne and I were aware, as was he, that our good-byes might be our last. The Indian summer of old age was over for him. Winter, be it brief or long, was the only season left.

We also gave much thought to him because of his example. Jacobo had drunk from the same small stream nearly all his life, yet he had grown beyond any danger of becoming like the dipper. He, too, had left the village when necessary, but had always come back. We were certain we would too.

The task of the student is not to copy the teacher but to apply things taught to what is needed. We needed adventure now, new horizons, which he understood. Even in his eighties, he still relished new experience, still had an appetite for travel. If he and Liza visited their daughter in Denver, he insisted on riding as far to the back of the bus as he could find a seat. From there he observed everything that transpired: who got off, who got on, who used the restroom, who spoke to whom. From his lookout at the back he studied the dynamic of his temporary village on wheels. Among those he studied was his own wife, who opted for a

quieter and smoother ride, up front near the driver. Jacobo would have positioned himself similarly on airplanes, which he and Liza boarded on annual visits to other, more distant children, except for one problem. His thick fingers could not operate the buckles of the seatbelts. He was compelled to sit next to his front-row-loving wife, so that she could strap him in and let him out.

In late August, Anne and I piled most of what we owned on the back of the yellow truck, pulled a green tarp over the load, and headed out of the village looking like Okies exiting the Dust Bowl. We took our farmer's tans and scuffed boots across the hot plains to Austin, where everyone we met, it seemed, was sleekly bronzed and fluent in discussing semiotics. Our hands were calloused, and, we worried, maybe our minds and

manners were too. It was months before we lost our bumpkin shame and overcame the urge to flee.

That winter Alex called from El Valle to say Jacobo had elected to be baptized again. The news caught us by surprise, for we had rarely known Jacobo to go to church. He had been brought up Catholic, then switched, at least nominally, to Presbyterianism over the issue of his daughters' education, and later sampled other sects, including the Latter Day Saints. But organized religion never seemed to command much of his attention, let alone his faith. Now, however, in his eighty-second year he had pledged himself to become an *Adventista*, a Seventh Day Adventist, joining a church in Dixon that Liza attended. After certain preparations, he submitted to baptism by full immersion. It was one of the last occasions Alex photographed him.

Years earlier Alex had started photographing Jacobo almost by accident. The momentum of happenstance and other projects led him to the old man. From that point on, their relationship grew naturally, and the pictures were part of it. Now Alex stopped photographing him in the same gradual, unarticulated way. The visits continued as before, but now the camera stayed at home. One reason was that with the context of ranch work less available, the relationship necessarily shifted. But there were other reasons, too. "I guess part of it," Alex later said, "was I didn't want to show it. I didn't want to show the fire burning out." And so the negatives of Jacobo, filed away in binders and boxes, lay untouched, and the detritus of other projects piled on top of them.

Anne and I returned to the village the next summer, and the summer after that. On each trip we noticed changes in Jacobo. His voice grew quieter and more gravelly, as though his energy waned. We were more likely to find him in the kitchen than in the fields, and during our visits he tended to follow the conversation more than lead it. Especially when the group grew large, he receded into the background, leaving center stage to Liza and Lalo. No longer did the old man hold a roomful of listeners rapt with outrageous stories. He sat back from the table in an armchair beside the refrigerator and watched and nodded. As time passed, Alex, Anne, and I found ourselves referring to him more and more as *Jacobito*, in the diminutive, as though somehow he were shrinking.

There were only the three of us again, as Alex and Susan had split up. Many things at that time were seeming to go awry. I finished at Texas and tried, in vain, to get a job teaching in New Mexico. Anne and I decided we could not come back and live, as before, on nothing. We had a daughter now, responsibilities. I had to have work. Spirits heavy, we loaded yet another truck and headed the wrong direction: east to North Carolina, where I had landed a job with a conservation organization. It was a good job in a good place, but far from where we felt at home.

Alex continued to migrate annually between east and west, between the university and the village, and in 1982 someone new rode with him. Margaret Sartor, blond and bright, was also a photographer, and a book designer. They worked together on a book about a photographer from Chiapas, Mexico. Before the project was finished, they married. Margaret was soon accustomed to summers in El Valle and to visits with the old man, up the road, who was no longer a worker, who rarely strayed from porch and kitchen, but who always smiled to see her and warmly took her hand. It was in the course of Alex and Margaret's fourth trip west together, from somewhere near the Mississippi, that they stopped to telephone ahead to El Valle. Alex placed the call. He was told Jacobo had suffered a stroke. He had been taken to the hospital in Santa Fe but was not expected to recover.

"The night before he was talking with us here, just like you and me are talking now," said Lalo.

"He ate a good meal," Liza said, "and then he went to bed the same as always. But in the morning he did not get up for breakfast. I went to his door to call him. There was no answer, so I went in. I thought he was dead."

The ambulance took him first to Española. Liza thought he would be transferred to the hospital at Los Alamos, but the doctor said no, there was no brain surgeon there. So on he went to Santa Fe.

The doctors connected him to a respirator and other life-sustaining devices. Liza was advised that his heart or kidneys might fail, or if not, then she would have to decide when to disconnect the equipment. She said, "Not yet. We must wait for the rest of the family."

For three days the children and their families gathered, coming from as far away as West Germany and Guam. At last, all assembled, they met as a group with the doctor. One daughter said, "My daddy will come back." The doctor said, "If he does, he'll always be like this." They came to a decision: take away the machines.

He lived for four more days. The doctor told Liza he had never seen a heart so strong.

The phone rang, and it was Alex.

"It's over," he said.

"That's it, then."

"That's it."

There was a pause. In the long-distance buzz we could hear the faint but urgent sounds of someone else's conversation.

"Well," I said, "how is Liza holding up?"

"Okay, I guess. Under the circumstances."

"The funeral?"

"I'm not sure. They're still making arrangements."

"Wish I could be there."

"Yeah, me too." The phantom voices in the line jabbered on. Alex, kindly, didn't ask me why I didn't catch a plane and come, and I didn't want to explain. I wanted to be there, but by going, I feared I'd draw attention to myself. I worried I'd be perceived as someone who had come too far, acting like blood kin, when I was not. Probably I was wrong, but at the time I couldn't bring myself to see things differently.

Alex spoke again: "You know, driving out, after we heard about Jacobo, Margaret and I talked about the photographs I took of him. I think I've got a couple of boxes of just negatives around here somewhere."

"You took a lot."

"I don't know if they amount to much, but maybe there is something I could do with them. Maybe some kind of tribute."

"That would be good."

"You think there's anything you'd want to write?"

"I'll write Liza tonight."

"No, that's not what I mean. I mean, would you want to write something about Jacobo?"

"No chance with this job. There isn't time."

"Oh."

"Maybe on vacation I could, but honestly, I don't know how much longer we can keep on here. We've got to get back—and stay."

"Right."

You go out and walk down the road. You kick stones. You look at the sky. You see longer and deeper into the evening blue than you usually do. You find nothing, finally, to criticize in the sky or in events.

I did not keep a copy of the letter I wrote Liza that night. I no doubt said the expected things, which were no less true for being expected. I may even have said that I thought of Jacobo as the grandfather I'd never had, for both of mine had died before I'd been old enough to know them. I knew this was true for Anne and Alex as well, for we'd talked about it once.

I did not write of any memories of him, though many came to mind. They were memories of impish stories and sly grins, of early-morning whiskeys and stolen water. None was right to talk about now.

And I know I did not say that I was glad for him to have died when he had and how he had, that I was proud his last years had been as stoic as his life, free of complaint, focused, and clear. I didn't say that the last and possibly most important thing I had learned from watching him was what a hard job it was to die well. It required vast amounts of luck and strength, and he had been fortunate to possess both.

Jacobo had prepared. One had to believe he was reconciled when his time came. And then the stroke gave no pain and required no struggle. It granted time for the family to come together. And then life ended. If Jacobo could have planned it, he'd have planned it that way.

He died four days short of his eighty-seventh birthday, and his burial brought more people to the village than had gathered there in many, many years. Cars so choked the road by the *camposanto* that the movement of traffic in and out of the village entirely ceased, and the crowd spilled outside the pigwire fence of the graveyard and stretched back toward the road. Not least of the reasons for the unprecedented crowd was the size of the Romero family. At his death Jacobo had twelve children, forty-seven grandchildren, and thirty-five great-grandchildren. And they were joined on that clear June day by scores of cousins and other relations, *compadres* from the sheep camps, *politicos* from every corner of the county, and countless neighbors and friends. The day was yet more exceptional because Alex, a gringo, an outsider by birth, upbringing, and language, delivered the graveside eulogy.

None of our small group had heard of an Anglo presiding, even briefly, at such an event anywhere in the mountains.

There had been a memorial service the previous day at the church in Dixon, but the words said at that gathering had dealt with matters of salvation, with things cosmic, things meaningful mainly to the faithful.

There was scarcely mention of Jacobo the man. Alex and Margaret left the service disappointed.

Evidently some of the family shared their feelings. In fact a number of the grandchildren had felt excluded, for the proceedings had been entirely in Spanish. It was past midnight when Lalo and Michael Rogers, Louisa's son, called at the house Alex and Margaret had built overlooking the hayfield, not far from Anne's and mine. Alex rose from bed and groggily answered the door. Lalo and the grandson wanted to know if he would speak at the burial.

Alex struggled through the night, writing and rewriting, to find words of farewell. Early in the morning he went to the Romero house and asked to borrow Jacobo's Bible. He found the old man's bookmark at the Twenty-Third Psalm: "Yea, though I walk through the valley of the shadow of death. . . ."

The day was cloudless and dry—under other circumstances, a day for irrigating. Alex shaved and dressed. He and Margaret trudged up the dusty road. They had to pick their way through a maze of pickups and Pontiacs to reach the graveyard. Finally Alex stood, casket before him, beside the meticulously groomed funeral director who would introduce him.

Alex looked out on the faces of a crowd whose limits he could not see, a crowd filled with the faces of northern New Mexico: old people gumming their bridgework, faces leathery, eyes dim, exerting themselves just to stand and listen in the relentless sun; teen-age girls in floral blouses, wearing the darkest, most impenetrable of sunglasses, their wavy hair cascading round their faces; boys and young men, lean and athletic, the most restless in the crowd; and older men, some as strong as tractors, some puffy from drinking, some lean from weather and work, some twisted and wasting from car wreck, illness, or injury in the mines; and the women in their perms looking fresher than the men but no less marked by life and labor, their ring-heavy hands clasped before them, the skin of their hands showing better than their well-creamed faces the age and effort of their lives.

It was a crowd where few enjoyed the good looks of actors in the soaps, where no jaws jutted with senatorial self-confidence. People slouched, shuffled, stared back at the nervous gringo clutching a few damp pages, who obviously suffered from the heat in his dark suit with the trousers too short and dust coating his shoes. The funeral director introduced him, expressing surprise that an Anglo should speak over the grave of Jacobo Romero and saying, truer than he knew, that it was a sign of the man whose body lay before them that the two languages, English and Spanish, should both be heard on this occasion.

"There are many of you here at graveside that knew Jacobo far better than I did," Alex began. "At first I didn't think it was fitting for an outsider, someone who has lived here for only ten years, to have the honor of speaking here. But then I realized it was fitting. Because my bearing witness to the life of this man is symbolic of the man he was. He did not care about my race or my background, which were so different from his. What mattered was that I was his *vecino*, his neighbor and his friend."

Alex looked up from his notes and took heart in the faint nods he thought he saw, the wind-like murmurs of assent. In the manner of all funeral orators, he went on to memorialize the deceased's classic virtues, and unlike many others in his situation, he was fortunate that he did not have to invent them. His voice grew stronger as he spoke of the old man's dedication to hard work, to his family, his loyalty to his village, his political party, and his neighbors. He said Jacobo had been a teacher of important values, even to a city-raised *gabacho* like himself.

It was inappropriate, of course, to say how much the old man had delighted in irony, how he loved to shock people with the gruesome details of his stories, how on occasion he was as cruel as he was other times kind, as when he killed a nuisance dog with a hammer. Burials are no time for complexity, and Jacobo was a complex man. How else to explain the contrasts of that day—so many villagers, drawn from miles around, who by their numbers said that the dead man had embodied their idea of a villager's villager. And the curly-haired gringo, awkward, out-of-place, but now speaking with authority, because he felt the crowd agreeing with him, because he felt it was important to say that the man they were burying, judged by standards from outside the mountains, should be considered an important man, a man not just of the village, but of the world.

When the casket was lowered and the young men, fetching shovels from the corner of the fence, began to cover it with earth, Alex, like everyone, joined the line of mourners paying respects to the family. He was told they liked what he had said.

He walked home following the same path that storm water travels
when it washes from the graveyard to our field. He thought of the irony of
his situation: that he would have liked to photograph the burial, the
enormous crowd, the clotted road. He'd have set his camera atop the hill.
But the photograph hadn't happened, because he had been in it. As he
walked he felt the anxieties of the long night and difficult day ebb from
him, satisfied he'd done his best for his friend. He passed the tree where
we'd hung the plastic rose, and he thought about looking for it, but he had
not slept and his nerves still jangled, and he was expected at the Romero
house, where there'd be a lunch for all the village.

Feeding Canto

*The sound of a cow eating has two parts: cuh-*wrump, *teeth bite and slide,* cuh-*wrump,* bite and slide. *Hardworking teeth, grinding by sliding, day after day. It is nothing to think about. Cows are beasts: you grow them to kill them, or sell them for someone else to kill. Their teeth have nothing to do with your teeth, if you have any.*

Eating is the work of the cow, feeding the work of the man. Listen to them: cuh-*wrump,* bite and slide, cuh-*wrump. The snow mutes the far sounds, the truck on the road, the chain saws up the valley, the wind behind the ridge. And the near sounds come closer, like a whisper in your ear. You hear the huff of cowbreath as mist jets from the nostrils. The hay rustles as you spear it with the fork. You toss it, pivoting low, like swinging a scythe in the old days. Dry snow creaks under the big* *red legs. Pink nostrils stretch out for odors of food. And then a shake of the head tears the hay pads apart, and the teeth begin, cuh-*wrump.

The muffled chorus of huffs and sliding teeth belongs to you, along with the heat of the red-haired backs and the wet animal breath that smells of forgetfulness and slime. This is the lung smell that each October lies behind the reek of fat and offal when you butcher, and which you will smell again from the carcass of the spot-cheeked one, the fencebreaker, who drops her calves in thickets, who feeds coyotes. You may soon enough smell it from her, depending.

To you belong the discarded hides behind the killing place, where magpies pick them clean. And to you belong the yearlings' horns, the notches of ear flesh, and the balls of the bull calves. Yours is the blood-covered, shit-slick work of the corral, but you also possess, equally, the labor of feeding in this moment in the quiet confidential snow.

Breathing deep the river-water taste of the air, you swing the fork, wide and low, spreading the food so the weakest calf has room to eat. The skin of your face is thick with cold, but the cold does not go deep. Soon enough you will have coffee and a wood fire under a snow-laden roof. You do not hurry.

Awake in your bed last night you heard the wind, which painted snow on the sides of the fence posts. Then morning came, as calm as a benediction. Before the others, you rose and dragged the bales with the hook.

Time, in this moment, does not pass. This is the moment between moments, when the snow on the roof does not slide from the eaves, when the door of the outhouse neither rattles nor creaks, when the fence posts do not groan against the nails and wire that you forced upon them, that your father forced upon them, and your sons and the women of your family for years have forced upon them.

This is the moment which you command, when snow clings to the branches of the cottonwoods, when you swing the fork and the mind of the spot-cheeked cow is flooded with appetite, when old age has strength and red-haired beasts find nourishment, and when you and the spot-cheeked one, in your particular and separate ways, prevail.

Acknowledgments

The authors wish to acknowledge the generous advice and assistance of Anne deBuys, Michael Godfrey, Beth Hadas, Iris Tillman Hill, Helen Lucero, Ed Ranney, and Margaret Sartor.

They would especially like to thank the Lyndhurst Foundation whose support and encouragement made this book possible. The John Simon Guggenheim Memorial Foundation provided assistance during the period when the majority of photographs were made. Almost a decade later the Duke Institute of the Arts helped to subsidize the printing of these images.

They wish to express their gratitude also to Eloisa and Olivario Romero, Faby and Jim Skaggs, Louisa and Norm Rogers, and to all the Romero family. Thanks to one and all.

Books mentioned in the text include:

Robert Coles and Alex Harris. *The Old Ones of New Mexico*. Albuquerque: University of New Mexico Press, 1973, 1989.

―――. *The Last and First Eskimos*. Boston: New York Graphic Society, 1979.

William deBuys. *Enchantment and Exploitation: The Life and Hard Times of a New Mexico Mountain Range*. Albuquerque: University of New Mexico Press, 1985.

Alex Harris and Margaret Sartor, eds. *Gertrude Blom: Bearing Witness*. Chapel Hill: The University of North Carolina Press for the Center for Documentary Photography, Duke University, 1984.

238

This book was set in 11/15 Janson
by Keystone Typesetting, Inc.
Printed and bound in Japan
by Dai Nippon Printing Company Ltd.
Book designed by Margaret Sartor